The Compleat Observer?

Qualitative Studies Series

General Editor: Professor Ivor F Goodson, Faculty of Education, University of Western Ontario, London, Ontario, Canada, N6G 1G7

The Compleat Observer?
A field research guide to observation

Jack Sanger

 The Falmer Press

(A member of the Taylor & Francis Group)
London • Washington, D.C.

UK   The Falmer Press, 1 Gunpowder Square, London, EC4A 3DE
USA   The Falmer Press, Taylor & Francis Inc., 1900 Frost Road, Suite 101, Bristol, PA 19007

First published in 1996

A catalogue record for this book is available from the British Library

Library of Congress Cataloging-in-Publication Data are available on request

ISBN 0 7507 0550 7 cased
ISBN 0 7507 0551 5 paper

Jacket design by Caroline Archer

Typeset in 10/12 pt Garamond by
Graphicraft Typesetters Ltd., Hong Kong

Printed in Great Britain by Biddles Ltd., Guildford and King's Lynn on paper which has a specified pH value on final paper manufacture of not less than 7.5 and is therefore 'acid free'.

Contents

For Jane, Joseph and Luke

Now for the Art of catching fish, that is to say, How to make a man that was none to be an Angler by a book, he that undertakes it shall undertake a harder task than Mr Hales, a most valiant and excellent fencer, who in a printed book called *A Private School of Defence* undertook to teach that art of science, and was laughed at for his labour. Not but that many useful things might be learned by that book, but he was laughed at because that art was not to be taught by words, but practice: and so must Angling. And note also, that in this Discourse I do not undertake to say all that is known, or may be said of it, but I undertake to acquaint the Reader with many things that are not usually known to every Angler; and I shall leave gleanings and observations enough to be made out of the experience of all that love and practise this recreation to which I shall encourage them. For Angling may be said to be so like the Mathematicks, that it can never be fully learnt; at least not so fully, but that there will still be more new experiments left for the trial of other men that succeed us.

Izaak Walton 1593–1683
The Compleat Angler

1 Problems and Pitfalls

The Aristotelian tradition also held that one could work out all the laws that govern the universe by pure thought: it was not necessary to check by observation. (Hawking, 1988)

It was not until 1980, thirty-seven years after being born, that I first realized that there was a world of difference between seeing and observing. All those years I had found my way around with unconscious lack of precision, only observing when I needed to remember a route, or a page for an exam or the face of someone who might turn out to be important to me. I was a doctoral student, in a classroom in London, supposedly in search of the way that teachers introduce complex concepts to learners. I remember vividly the sense of frustration of wondering when and how I might be able to record a complex concept. It was as though I was one of those lead-lined receptacles deep beneath the earth's surface, filled with a liquid which would capture the momentary path of a neutrino as it winged its way through matter. A section of my notes for the event, looked like this:

Snippets of conversation drift by and attract my attention. 'A mate of mine fell forty feet off a tree on Saturday . . .'

The two girls next to me are doing graphs for mathematics' homework. One says, 'Oh I see . . . !' She corrects her homework. Peer teaching. A sign, a further sign, of the bond between them. They touch regularly. They talk a great deal and share private jokes. Their eyes meet and they smile. They dress almost identically in pale green V-necked jumpers and blue jeans. Watches. Necklaces. Hairstyles.

The teacher begins to read out two poems, by Rupert Brooke and James Kirkup. She reads the former. The two girls read and follow. The class is quiet. While the group answers questions and discuss phrases, descriptions, images of an idyllic England, the two girls remain stoically silent staring at the words, eyes refusing contact with the teacher while their fingers fiddle with their ornaments.

Decoding the poems' meanings takes place through dialogue between the teacher and individuals — whoever can manage the act of analysis. The teacher is always part of the dialogue and the pupils have at best only partial participation. Most learning is by proxy and by later emulation. The bulk of first hand learning will take place in different surroundings — those of their own homes or the backs of buses or in the library. In the classroom the **stage** metaphor tends to take hold of the observer's understanding. A few of the class have gradually assumed prominent roles in dialogue with the teacher. For the rest of them there are walk on parts or audience passivity.

One pupil says of the first poem, 'People don't think like that any more.' It becomes a lost statement, trapped in mid-air between the teacher's need to hurry on with her own line of knowledge and the clamour of other offerings. The girl next to me writes a note to her friend. I can't see what she is writing.

The second poem seems to induce a shock of recognition. It is a simpler, cruder, more aggressive statement. The teacher leads the group (willingly on their part) into an agreement with the poet's statements . . . and then begins to unpack meanings. She offers a belated aside, 'Oh, put a full stop at the end of the first line. The typist missed it out.'

The girl next to me does this for her friend, too, with a smile. She completes her note and folds it into an aeroplane. Then she unfolds it and places it under the poem. In the classroom a girl is suspecting the author of not really knowing the reality of war. Meanwhile, the girl next to me has placed a small hand mirror against her bag. She does not appear to want to stare at it but catches the occasional reflection of herself in a less aware state. She suddenly sits up and smiles. An expression of recognition when she hears the teacher say . . . 'Children often say to their parent, "I didn't ask to be born!"'

A chuckle runs round the class. There is a feeling of identification with the statement. There is more discussion of the poem and Jesus dying for Mankind. The girl next to me checks her bangles. The atmosphere in the room is more electric as the discussion covers the act of dying for a cause: hunger strikers in Northern Ireland, suffragettes . . . The girls beside me become animated with each other but they talk in whispers.

A girl says she would die to save two others but not one. The last line of the poem says, 'Only nothing is worth dying for.' The class reject this without any dissension. The teacher gives an interpretation. That there is no purpose to life. She introduces 'nihilistic' as a term. The lesson never discusses the quality of the poetry and therefore never moves towards a critical awareness of its authority. The insertion of a comma is like the appending of QED to a theorem.

The lesson completed, I manage to retrieve the girl's words from the waste bin. I wanted confirmation of her own idiosyncratic hidden agenda of learning. The note read: 'THAT MAN HAS WRITTEN TWO FULL PAGES AND IN THIS LESSON — ABOUT WHAT WE ARE DOING. HE'S WRITING NON-STOP HE MUST BE BORED OUT OF HIS MIND.'

Afterwards I talk to the teacher in the staffroom. I feel elated at my acute observation of the two girls and the irony of the note. But the teacher tells me that a boy, in full view of the class, gave her a present at the start of the session. An apple. She was invited to squeeze it but refused. She gave it back. He squeezed. A plastic penis burst through a hole. The present was from ex-pupils, now at university. The same perpetrators have written on the boy's piece of work, 'Poor work. Not surprising, considering the teacher'. These ex-offenders left five years previously but the memory of the teacher seems to have remained, undiminished.

It was only when I began to reflect upon my notes did I realise that observation and seeing were two different activities which, though obviously connected, nevertheless conflicted. Just as Britain and America are said to be divided only by language, so observation and seeing are divided only by the desire to perceive.

What did I see and what did I observe? Well, I observed some of the goings on between the two girls next to me. I observed bits and pieces of the teacher interacting with pupils, What I **saw** is not in the notes. Maybe it registered for some brief, indeterminate length of time in my short term memory before being dumped in the bin labelled 'insignificant'. We obviously circumnavigate the world by seeing, primarily, and become trained to do it without too much thought, relegating much of our visual mapping of our environment to the hind brain. Observation is brought on by the stimulus to be necessarily aware. Finding our way in a strange town. Being faced by the trauma of a hospital visit. Walking through a dangerous precinct. Or by doing research. If the actions we are engaged in are significant to us, then we slip the gear of seeing and engage observation.

How did I come to observe what I did? Because it was part of the contract I had with my researching self? However, this contract involved selection based on the naiveté of my understanding. And, therefore, the denial of other classroom activities. It was as if the particular focus of observation had been forced upon me. No subtle, informed and experienced Sherlock Holmes, here, such as is found in the following dialogue from *Silver Blaze* by Conan Doyle and quoted by Zizek (1991).

'Is there any point to which you wish to draw my attention?'
'To the curious incident of the dog in the night.'
'The dog did nothing in the night.'
'That was the curious incident,' remarked Holmes.

Notions of observing the absence of something never even occurred to me at this time! Indeed, my interest in absence came a few years later, once I began to read Barthes, Foucault, Eco, Derrida and Lacan.

If it was complex concepts I was after, why didn't I home in on the teacher's introduction of 'nihilism', rather than being magnetized by the cloning girls next to me? Was it an unconscious heuristic leap back to adolescence, when such girls were on the other side of the classroom, remote and mysterious? Was I exploring the hidden curriculum? Was I case-studying two learners as they were being taught — now known as 'pupil-pursuit'? Was I making conscious selection of observational subjects or was the whole process prejudiced by unknown, unconscious Freudian drives?

Doing observation for professional purposes is not as easy as it at first appears. Far from being a first line of defence in the search for objectivity, it can be a leaky, permeable membrane. One which allows as much to issue from the observer as hits her wall of consciousness from the outside with that satisfying but deceptive thump of factuality. The key motif in much art and philosophy, not to mention psychology, is that of the observer seeking and discovering aspects of the self in the Other. By the Other, I mean that which is outside, novel, strange or unknown. An image which sums it up is Escher's drawing of an eye staring back at the viewer (*Eye, Mezzotint, 1946*), in whose pupil is the reflection of the viewer, only the image is that of a skull. I, the observer, searching for fundamental truths about the nature of existence and my own mortality.

And yet? Isn't there a place for the kind of research illuminated by my early classroom notes, where the eye roams in apparent random and the moving finger writes what it will? There are a 1001 stories in any half-hour in the classroom and this is just one that the net drags in. It depends, researchers would say, on who your audience is. And what kind of research you are doing. Sometimes these amount to the same thing.

We write for an audience; ourselves or one or more significant others. We, likewise, observe for an audience. And, in the main, we are reconstructing what we see for this audience, whether we do it through the medium of oral recall, video-tape or notes.

My field notes probably wouldn't satisfy a scientist but they might prove interesting to a teacher, a journalist, a naturalistic enquirer or a phenomenologist . . . they might help to stimulate a discourse. And making people think may be more important to me than pinning down what a scientist might regard as objective truth. Thus, observation may be inextricably tied to a sense of its eventual use. The processes of planning, selecting, ordering and eventually recording events may determine what we observe in the first place.

The field notes also tell us something about the complexity of time. Events that were occurring in the classroom were related to events five years previously. A contingency was being revealed, though not to me. Had I not talked to the teacher I would never have known about the apple incident in the classroom, anyway, never mind its historical antecedents. We blithely talk about case study, for example, being representatives of instances in time. But the effects of historical contingency may be less than palpable.

As for myself, this observer of life as it is happening, what of me and my fly on the wall role? Blissfully unaware of the major event at the front of the class, I sat in a seat in one corner at the back, attempting a covert recording of significant proceedings. A bit like a Star Trek captain, intending to have no effect upon a culture I was visiting. The girl's note is a salutary reminder that invisibility is more fantasy than reality for the observer. We can minimize our effect but would be foolish to claim that we have no effect at all.

Observation is a slippery business. The world is exponentially messier than a laboratory and the latter has proven more ambiguous and error-strewn than science would ever admit. Just this one set of well-meant field notes have thrown up validity problems which include the history underpinning events, the biography of the observer and the nature of selection of events to witness. And we haven't begun to look at the language of recording yet!

Foreground and Background

Nazruddin crosses the border between two countries with his donkey and his cart of straw. He never returns by this route. The chief of the border guards notices that Nazruddin looks wealthier at each crossing and suspects him of smuggling. One day he orders the straw to be searched. There is nothing to be found. Another day he has the straw cut up into tiny pieces. Nothing. Yet another day he has the straw burned. Nothing. A further day he boils the straw. No evidence. Embarrassed, he gives up and watches Nazruddin grow rich enough to retire. Years later he meets the wealthy Nazruddin in a beautiful part of the country, outside his large white house. He asks him whether he was smuggling something across the border. Nazruddin smiles and says that he was. The chief of the border guards asks what. 'Donkeys!' laughs Nazruddin.

Sometimes, observation falls foul of the same false logic as that used by the chief of the border guards. We look where we expect to find rather than opening ourselves to any possibility that might turn up. For the chief, the donkey was too every day a creature, too obviously part of life's continuing **background**, to be significant. Despite the fact that it was a major aspect of his observational picture, he merely saw it and did not observe it.

Key features in the process of observation seem to be **foreground** and **background**. There is overwhelming evidence to the effect that human cognition adopts a patterning approach to the potentially chaotic data which confronts it, every moment of the waking day. At all times the brain functions to create order among the ·deluge of signals reaching it (Vernon, 1970). It observes what the mind-set requires it to observe. Donkeys become invisible.

We always have to ask ourselves whether we are looking in the right place for what we want to find. And in the right way.

> Nazruddin was found by his neighbour one night, on hands and knees under the light, outside his house. The neighbour, too, dropped on all fours. He asked what Nazruddin had lost and was told that the old man had mislaid his house key. After an hour's search, nothing was found. The neighbour asked Nazruddin where he had last seen the key. 'Over there, in the bushes.' 'Then why are we looking here?' Nazruddin smiled cagily 'Because there is no light over there to find anything.'

Apart from looking in the wrong place, this story emphasizes that the observational technique, itself, needs to be questioned. The 'light' in the story may be analogous to the observational instrument by which we hope to capture an elusive aspect of the social world. A checklist, a questionnaire, an interaction analysis chart may make you feel as though you are shedding light on research's mysterious 'field' but actually, you may find only pebbles and no key. Too much observational — and other — research, merely confirms its instrumentation rather than uncovering anything significant.

Significance

It's a powerful concept. It speaks of the authority of judgment. It suggests a hierarchy in which it, itself, is near the top and *triviality* is at the bottom. For neophyte researchers, it is an early burden. They go off into the social world, live with mysterious peoples or enter the laboratory, and wrestle with the anxiety that what they are doing may, in the end, have little significance.

Perhaps we can tie together the three terms we have been exploring so far: foreground, background and significance. Since it appears that what we place in the foreground is what we want to observe, then it follows that what we find in our foreground is what we deem to be significant. A simplistic thought, perhaps. But it leads to a fundamental axiom of research, namely:

> Information is that which an individual perceives as significant. (Sanger, 1985)

In other words, all the data which is barraging us, second by second, is sieved through for what we want or need at any moment. This is how we become informed. In the main, we apply our conscious or unconscious screen of significance to data, taking from it what becomes our information. Occasionally this may be overridden by powerful external signals which we have to respond to, in order to avoid injury, for example, but usually the process ticks along without us necessarily being aware of it.

Take a look at what follows, in the box. Have a go at counting the typographical 'fs' that you find there. In other words, for each F or f, you get a point. Allow yourself ten to twenty seconds. Later, ask one or two others to do the same. You may not have the same answer and you may not have the correct answer, anyway!

Count the Fs

The significance that we attach from today to Friday's Great Education Reform Bill as a matter of great concern to the scientific community of physicists, chemists and all students of the inside of the atom.

(The correct answer can be found at the foot of the next page)

Now, how do you account for you, or your friends, not managing to arrive at the correct answer? If you did, fine, But when I set this exercise to would-be professional observers, it actually is rare for anyone to come up with the right answer. Indeed, I can predict with certainty that most people will be clustered around a solution of six fs. There are a number of hypotheses that my groups come up with to account for their corporate lapse:

- overlooking the insignificant or trivial word 'of' whenever it occurs;
- reading phonics make 'of' sound like 'ov' so you miss the soft f' sound;
- the time factor leads to stress;
- the exercise seems so simplistic, you don't try or you look for devious catches that aren't there;
- you only read by scanning nouns, verbs and adjectives.

And so on. Hypotheses to account for error? In fact, it is the perfect exercise to differentiate bias from error. Error is the consequence of a mistake. Bias is the consequence of an in-built disposition to see, hear, taste, smell, touch or do things in a particular way.

You may well ask what the observer can do to counteract this disposition. What I ask my groups to do is to read the lines backwards, looking for each f. Or read them upside down. In each case, use a pencil point to mark off each f. Up shoot the scores. You can try now, if your answer was less than the correct solution. Why does this prove more effective? In the first attempt, perhaps we go through all the motions of reading. It's a habit, a ritual, to approach text in a particular way. We can't get out of it that easily.

Even Though We Aren't Reading for Meaning!

By asking people to count the fs, they forego meaning, relegating it down their hierarchy of significance. Most of them have no idea what the passage was about, after the exercise.

A major difference between seeing and observing is that the observer takes steps to counteract the in-built biases we all possess. Just as the text is turned upside down to make it unfamiliar, the observer turns the world on its head to make it unfamiliar. The cliché for this is 'making the commonplace exotic'. Thus, ethnomethodologists might look at nurses' log books to see how they account for their professional world. If the accounts omit large parts of their every day world, is it because it has become too familiar for them to see any more? It took a television documentary by Roger Graef showing the Thames Valley police interviewing rape victims to bring public pressure on all police to change their interview methods. Until then, the police, themselves, could not see the oppressive bias in their actions — and they had cleared the documentaries for public viewing on the assumption that the practice I was witness to, was perfectly acceptable. I once talked to a policeman who regarded himself as a non-sexist professional. I showed him the cartoons pinned up on the canteen notice board. He was embarrassed because he hadn't thought of them in that light! They were just jokes. The methods we use to counteract our biases are the instruments of observation. We will explore some of them later as individual methods of accounting for the world, or as combined approaches to get at the truth, as people understand it.

Postscript

I asked a woman friend once, who was a self-professed sceptic about all things supernatural, what she would do if an alien space craft landed in her garden. 'I wouldn't even see it'. she said!

We have to work hard to see with new eyes, or with the eyes of others. Otherwise our very familiarity with the environment blinds us to perspicacity.

> Just after Christmas in 1648 John Aubrey, out hunting with some friends, rode through the Wiltshire village of Avebury and there saw a vast prehistoric temple, the greatest of its age in Europe, which up to then had been undiscovered. It was not hidden in some remote and desolate spot, for a thriving village stood within its ramparts, nor at that date was it particularly ruinous. Yet Aubrey was the first of his age to notice it. (Michell, 1973)

Between the two, error is the more visible enemy of observation, bias is the undercover agent.

* In the realm of factual truth there are 10 fs in the box on the page preceding this one.

2   'You Are Here!'

Becoming a researcher is too often like becoming a pupil in an exotic, hybrid school, the result of a cross between the worst of Eton and Dotheboys Hall. You may find yourself suffering from the elitist belief that what your research centre practises is methodologically superior to that of other centres, thus guaranteeing you a place in the sun and influence on your country's social policy for years to come. At the same time you may discover that you are dependent on small bowls of sustenance from those who head the centre, that more than this is not forthcoming and that your criticism of existing paradigms or novel methodological strategies at such places may result in your bowl being confiscated.

Slightly facetious perhaps but it points up the fact that researchers are trained to do the job and that much of that training places them at a particular point on a historically evolving map. For some neophytes, coming to research straight after school and university, the possibility of being anything other than a clone within the accepted orthodoxy of the research centre is negligible. For those for whom the training comes mid-working life, an uncomfortable time may lie ahead, with conflicts abounding between the centre's models and strictures concerning the ethics and practice of research and neophytes' common sense derived from the world of work and other experience.

It is an irony that a human activity which apparently prizes such notions as disinterest, objectivity, freedom from bias and the need for supportive evidence, should so often be blinkered in its training processes. Social science is divided into many camps, each of which has its own defined orthodoxy. This suggests a process of territorialism and the invention of differences, at play. The study of human behaviour may be superficially differentiated in many ways. But it comprises a limitless territory of ideas about the nature of lived experience which is continually being fought over by those who benefit from sovereignty over areas of it. For Foucault (1989), this study of human behaviour is a relatively late arrival on the scene of cultural aspiration, constituting a nineteenth and twentieth century enterprise. He argues that despite superficial differences, the underlying order which helps to create our visions of our own selves and behaviours, has a commonality and is highly regulatory. It may not be surprising then, to find more resemblance in the underlying social science enquiry, than difference.

When I first arrived for training in research, I had no clear conceptions of the philosophy which underpinned the centre's work, nor for that matter did

I have any clear idea about what social science was. Between then and now I have veered between feeling I have a clearer picture and feeling that there is no such possibility. Despite the thousands of hours of interviewing, observing, analyzing and writing, my mind refuses to create easily accessible compartments which truly differentiate one research approach from another. Nor does a clearly defined model advertise itself. In the event, I became an experienced researcher without what some might regard as the necessary explicit ballast of theoretical orthodoxy to keep me pointed in the right direction.

The Centre for Applied Research in Education (CARE), University of East Anglia, was a place in those days, which made a virtue out of unorthodoxy. Social science research into education was a growing field. The resultant vibrancy of new research territories being formed and novel methods being invented or, more likely, imported and renamed, gave that time a special flavour. If you wanted to be doing goal-free evaluation or if you wanted to be a research artist, fine (Parlett and Hamilton *et al*, 1977). If you wanted to employ fiction, well why not? (Walker, 1982) The prevailing doctrine was of liberal progressivism, underwritten by the democratic intent.

Before I took up research I was a trained and practising teacher and then a residential social worker in a therapeutic community dealing with emotionally disturbed adolescent girls. As a professional in both fields, I had to observe and record my observations. As time went on, my implicit theories concerning the research process have become more explicit but they don't appear to conform to any particular school of social science. They certainly haven't imprisoned me in a particular way of seeing. They seem to be essentially driven by practicability and utility. If they lack validity in some eyes at some time, that is in the nature of things. The defence for these falls from grace may have lain in attempts to achieve efficacy rather than total accuracy, in being clear and communicable rather than comprehensive and turgid, or in trying to stimulate discourse rather than invent a new rubric. However, as most researchers privately agree, the overriding reason why clear procedures don't seem to crystallize is that the world is a messy, non-clinical place and it's difficult to do clean research when there's that much mess around. It may be better in such conditions to produce the best evidence available with the resources at hand, admit the shortcomings but add fuel to debate. In some cases this will counteract decision-makers' reliance upon gut rhetoric or crude ideology. Or their reliance upon research, whose protocols, whilst theoretically sound, deliver nothing that offers a critique of the political or social issues at stake, never mind resolving them. Again, it may offer counteraction to commonly held myths among the population.

What I found myself doing in those early research days, was marching under an ethnographic research banner called 'naturalistic enquiry'. Inside the marching throng, it looked to us all as though we hardly agreed on anything. Outside, though, people would see you as part of a tight-knit community with a very specific brief and shared philosophy (Barton and Lawn, 1980). I had arrived in the research milieu at a point when fragmentation into schools, approaches, tendencies and methodologies was accelerating. All within a vague stance of anti-positivism or anti-scientism. A non-comprehensive list of names for these schools include ethnography, naturalistic enquiry, ethnomethodology, symbolic interactionism, hermeneutics, case study, qualitative research, discourse analysis, social anthropology and latterly semiology. The terms blur with each other and perhaps only the exponents within each can happily differentiate at all how they contrast with the others. In the discourse which follows, ethnography or naturalistic enquiry are the terms commonly used to point the reader towards the qualitative research backcloth to observation and away from the quantitative or positivistic approaches.

Naturalistic enquiry must not be confused with scientific naturalism. Paradoxically, it must be more closely identified with anti-naturalism. Popper (1972) calls scientific approaches 'naturalistic' whereas Guba and Lincoln (1981) and most modern-day ethnographers regard naturalistic research as anti-positivist! How the term came to be used in its ethnographic version is hard to understand but in its present form, naturalistic enquiry seems a rather late coterminous descriptor for certain forms of ethnography where the accent is upon maintaining a posture of deference to the language, perceptions and actions of those who comprise the study. The label 'naturalistic' in educational enquiry would therefore signal that the research has been conducted in an educational milieu and seeks to characterize participant activity within programmes, projects or other settings.

The Split in Social Sciences: Positivism and Naturalism

How had it all culminated in this, for some, disagreeable pottage? It may be best to think of two images. One is a fairly natural looking tree. The other is a stylized, geometrical model of a tree. The former retains all the characteristics of a tree; the rough bark, the twisting branches, moments of asymmetry, scar tissue. The other is perfectly balanced, from leaf to root tip. No-one could mistake the second tree for a real one, but everyone knows what it represents. In order to produce the second tree, much detail is smoothed away. Information is reduced to produce basic shapes. The result can be reproduced at will. It can be played with, at an abstract level. It is like a computerized, mathematical symbol. Forests can be built with it as a basic unit. Our two trees represent two ways of visualizing methods for understanding social events. The former tries to recreate the reality as it was understood at the time, in all its complexity. The latter seeks such data from social events, as can be verified by stringent tests for objectivity. With the resulting information, reconstructed pictures of social events can take place: they can be manipulated and extrapolations can occur. The attempts to reproduce the natural tree founder as a result of naturalistic methods' difficulty in producing a tree which enables us to predict the shape of a copse, never mind a' forest. The development of the mathematical model of the tree can result in the basic problem that the forests it generates look even more removed from life than the original tree.

The second, scientifically modelled (positivistic) tree has a long history of antecedents which culminated, at the movement's peak, in the logical positivism of the 1930s and 40s. It had a great impact on social science because it appeared to offer a logically reduced framework of laws and behaviours for research which would provide a secure and irrefutable means of creating knowledge of the social world. It produced approaches still pervasive today such as survey methods, experimental and quasi-experimental research and statistical modelling. Whereas in the late nineteenth century and early twentieth century, disputes were not about numbers being an inadequate basis for social description and analysis, but about which practical method might be most appropriate, the gap since then has widened (Hammersley and Atkinson, 1983) and criticism has focused on weaknesses in positivistic methods' epistemological characteristics.

Hammersley and Atkinson cite Cohen and Wartofsky (1983) and Giddens (1979) in their inventory of weaknesses in the would-be scientific approach to research. In the first place, physical science is used as a model for methodological approaches, with its logic of experiment and the manipulation of variables in order to identify the relationships between them. People's behaviours, feelings and attitudes are subjected to scrutiny under laboratory conditions, where exacting lengths are undergone to achieve the same conditions for each individual under investigation. Where possible, the specific focus of the study is isolated from other, possibly contaminating influences. Outside the laboratory, attempts are made to reproduce the uncontaminated essence of laboratory work with control groups, careful sampling techniques and pre and post-testing procedures. In terms of doing observation this means having pre-structured observational items, categories, grids, stop watches and so on.

The second characteristic of the quasi-scientific approach is the appeal to universal laws governing human behaviours which posit regular relationships between variables that hold good across all circumstances. These can be systematized and made statistical.

A third area which is significant to these schools of thought, concerns the neutrality of research language and the invisibility of the researcher. Borrowing from the physical sciences again, only that which is directly observable can be held to be fact. Theory is preserved upon authenticated footings. Since this approach evolved against a philosophical, not to mention sub-atomic physical science world which was going relativist, there was increased concern over the arbitrariness of language, Saussure (Culler, 1976; Wittgenstein, 1953) and later, Derrida (Norris, 1987; Barthes, 1977). Consequently, emphasis was placed upon the standardization of procedures of observation. Measurements or data would derive from a stable, neutral, fact-focused language. Structured approaches, with pre-determined categories would support the researcher out there in the world with the security of disinterested even-handedness.

As a researcher I had no problem in rejecting these approaches. Hadn't my working experience shown that language was continually being reconstructed? Weren't people inconsistent and often volatile? Weren't there as many stories of an event as people taking part in it? It wasn't so much that as a therapist you would wish to get people to agree on what happened but rather you would get them to agree on a productive account of what happened so that they could move on. Use the experience if they needed to. Objectivity gives way to expediency. Not an easy concept to integrate into a research framework but more in tune with applied research and development than pure research.

The methods of the physical sciences, usually abbreviated to 'scientific method', have been assumed by the positivist school to be equally applicable to social phenomena (Toulmin, 1972). Scientific method presupposes the testing of theory, with a sharp distinction being made between the context of discovery and the context for validity, or justification (Reichenbach, 1938). The value of a theory grows, in these circumstances, from its robustness in standing the attempts to falsify it (Popper, 1972). An inherent value could thus be seen in standardizing all aspects of research so that replication can be formally monitored: whether it be the questions asked in surveys, the structure of interviews or the classification of observable events. From such a perspective the operations involved in most ethnographic studies would be regarded as untestable and, therefore, untenable. They would not provide sound causal links between observable events. Of course, from a phenomenological perspective, causal links do not necessarily constitute a desirable goal in theory building, anyway. Here, contingency and the singularity of experience, dominate. Comprehensive detail of the case comes before generalization to other circumstances. From Comte (1978) to Popper, the predisposition of social scientists in the scientistic tradition, has been to eliminate the possibilities of ambiguity and advance claims which would be acceptable to their physical science colleagues. The value for ethnographic approaches in positivist logic is in the insistence upon developing new forms of rigour which provide a sustainable basis for an enquiry into the natural context of the social world, where post-event replays are too absurd to even imagine. Schutz (1967) saw this dichotomy of outlooks as falling into two discrete rationalities, the scientific and the every day. For Schutz, the everyday remained problematic. Beyond the calling of the social scientist.

Obviously this does little to bridge the gap between research which owes its antecedence to phenomenology and research which is founded on the physical sciences. Bohm (1980) and Gauld and Shotter (1977) explore this dichotomy from the point of view of how human action is treated in the two rationales. Bohm uses the striking images of the hologram and the photograph to explain the difference in outlook. Schutz' social scientist essentially takes photographs of the world, focusing the camera on exactly what has been predetermined, by theory, as significant. What results is ripped out of the continuum of existence and contains none of the internal relations which pervade that existence. Cut a piece off the image and you cannot piece together the full photograph. Whereas a hologram shard, if broken off, still retains the whole image in itself. Bohm suggests that scientific method atomises the world into handleable unitary parts, whereas what is needed is a comprehension of the holistic integrity of its existence. The former, he calls 'the explicate order' and the latter, 'the implicate order'. The explicate order artificially screens out the mess of life, the implicate order attempts to deal with it in all its complexity.

Ethnography and Naturalistic Enquiry

We live in an intersubjectively constructed everyday world. It is the world researchers encounter daily and about which they must try to make sense. Because the variables in social life cannot be adequately controlled since they occur in such quantity and at so many levels with many of them lying outside the knowledge of the researcher, anyway, the ethnographic researcher nevertheless has to show that s/he is attempting to account for them. This accounting has a tradition that goes back through Weber, Dilthey and Kant but more recently, Winch (1958) attempts to resolve some of the dispute by drawing close parallels between social science and philosophy. He argues that, unlike positivism, both seek for intelligible connections between people, objects and events. He projects the world as being *non real* and therefore not suited to science's premises and protocols. In response to this argument, Bhaskar (1979) argues that the subject matter under study should determine the research methods we use to investigate that subject. Taking scientific enquiry as being a three-part process whereby the researcher-theorist identifies phenomena, constructs explanations for them and tests them, thus leading to a focus upon the generative mechanisms which produced them, Bhaskar sees the research process as leading the researcher from the manifest to the underlying structures of social understanding. Without this approach, we are stranded as beings in a society. Positivism would have us being bits and pieces in a game whose rules are beyond us. Naturalism would have us knowing ourselves, introspectively but falling short of contextual explanations of what is beyond us because our accounting becomes so subjective.

For Blumer (1969) the argument is about whether procedures employed to understand the social world are suited to that task and are not, in effect, self-fulfilling vehicles of understanding. That is, a mere underwriting of existing theories. The conscious application of theory to the social world may be a problem for highly structured scientistic approaches in research. The unconscious imposition of theory upon the social world is a central problematic of naturalistic enquiry approaches, despite attempts to be value-free. Fidelity to the perceptions of persons under study rather than to pre-existing methods and protocols leads to an approach which seeks to represent the lived experience of those under study. Whatever these individuals profess to believe in may not be *real* or acceptable, according to pre-existing theory, but it's real enough to those concerned and is real in its consequences for their future lives, (Thomas, 1919). Within naturalistic enquiry there may not be the same concern to exercise a unifying logic which stands outside the researcher and to which s/he can appeal, but a desire to show the boundaries within which social action is generated; often called the boundaries of the case and a major defining concept for case study.

From the perspective of qualitative research, social phenomena are seen as distinct from other phenomena of the natural world, whatever the methodology; symbolic interactionism, hermeneutics, ethnomethodology or ethnography. This is because social actors are seen to be inextricably both the products and the progenitors of society. As Bhaskar suggests, the individual arrives in the world with a society already formed to receive her and by her actions and the actions of others, society is transformed to receive others into it, in the same way. The dialectic is continuous. Society is in continuous change and social science will have to modify its methods, continually, to interpret it. At the heart of the ethnographic response to this shifting world, is the acceptance that as progenitors of our society we are well versed in reading much of its significance. We are cultural agents. The ethnographer is one who reflects upon being immersed in social events. This reflection upon immersion is brought into sharper focus when the ethnographer researches less familiar settings; say the sub-cultures of policing, nursing or teaching (Garfinkel, 1964; Cicourel and Kitsuse, 1963). Ethnomethodology has grown its research stance by interpreting sub-cultures via the analysis of how members of the sub-culture organize and account for their activities. Over-structured approaches to unfamiliar settings fall foul of the language, customs and behaviours implicit in them. There may be a case for surveys being based on extensive ethnographic immersion, but not without. The use of unstructured interviewing methods (MacDonald and Sanger, 1982), represents one way in which the ethnographer can gain access to the particular meanings implicit within sub-cultural behaviour. Observation often requires similar unstructured approaches (see chapter 8).

The ethnographer doesn't measure. The use of artificial conditions in clinical trials or rigid questioning techniques, presents subjects of a study with an environment which is perceived to be different from their natural milieu. It follows that their actions and perceptions could also be different. Generalizations about behaviour thus have a difficult problem to face if those generalizations cross the divide between the artificially simulated or constrained milieu and the natural (Harre and Secord, 1972; Cronbach, 1975). The strength of a naturalistic perspective lies in the acceptance of the singularity of the moment and the reliance upon third party audiences to make of the research, what they will. The observer becomes yet another variable entering the social dimension and by being included as part of the study (Norris and Sanger, 1984) accepts the significance of this entry. Neutrality is hardly a likely status for the researcher in a society which is so overwhelmingly political at every level. Some, (Becker, 1967; Gouldner, 1968) go so far as to see the research role as politically active, supportive of the oppressed. Others (MacDonald, 1977 and 1978) seek parity for all by evolving protocols which ensure that the disenfranchized have a voice, despite not having power over the funding of research.

When it comes to validity and generalization, naturalism and positivism stand head to head. These two research concepts tend to be central pillars in the development of theory, whatever the philosophic persuasion. To some extent they have been discussed already and a summary of the position reached earlier is that positivism leads to reductionism, reification, artificiality and non-generalizability to natural contexts. On the other hand naturalistic enquiry leads to lack of verification, overinterpretation and bias, and in some extreme circumstances, an almost wilful antagonism towards the concept of generalizability.

To counteract these weaknesses in naturalistic methods, attempts have been made to add rigour to its activities. Mess is accounted for, (Simons, 1980; Carr and Kemmis, 1983; Elliott, 1985), by **screening** in the variables. Triangulation of data gathering techniques and across a comprehensive population within the study, help to close the gap with the double blind approach, (Ford, 1975). Recognition of the power of grounded theory (Glaser and Strauss, 1967; Guba and Lincoln, 1981) and its inductive methodology leads to a closer tie between theory and practice. Mixed methodologies to counteract accusations of over-subjectivity should increase research validity (Fox and Hernandez-Nieto, 1981; Hammersley and Atkinson, 1983; Price, 1981).

Having established the need to ground theory in the changing context of the real world, it follows that observations made in that world should help to generate empirical insights, via progressive focusing and inductive reasoning, towards a conglomerating theory. The question asked is whether such theory has generalizable application. In Bhaskar's terms, how can real statements be made? To respond to this one must first differentiate between the fundamental attitudes to reality, as evidenced in positivism and naturalism. In the former, reality is grounded in a belief in the universal fact and in the latter it is grounded in historical fact: that is, it is grounded in a consensual viewpoint at a certain point in history. Thus, today we contrive to understand our world in terms of social forces and underpin such understandings with theory; Keynsian, Marxist, Freudian or whatever. Such theories are bounded by temporal parameters and social conventions, (Giddens, 1982). Generalizability can be adjudged, therefore, more in transformative than transferable terms. Scientific method would argue for transferability of understanding across cases, applications with some certainty. Naturalism explores cultural understandings, contexts and assumed realities. Generalization in this latter view is not the responsibility of the researcher but of the audience for it is through the dialectical process of engagement, reflection and action that knowledge becomes personalised, owned and transmuted. Indeed, Habermas (1972) argues, self-evidently, that self-reflection without action does not lead to social change. This view of critical reflection and social action had a strong influence on some forms of, particularly, naturalistic enquiry into educational issues. Drawing subjects under research scrutiny into a collaborative research process in order that they might gain a better purchase on the transformative process of social change, led some research practitioners (Stenhouse, 1975; Sanger, 1990) away from the grail of generalization and towards ownership, self-judgment and empowerment.

Educational Ethnography

The effects of this general rationale had its effects on educational research through the almost paradigmatic shifts of methodology, represented by the work of such as Jackson (1968) and Smith and Geoffrey (1968). They focused their work upon the detailed study of the minutiae of school interaction and had a prevailing concern to be open to new ways of researching that interaction. Theory was developed via the accumulation of insights developed on site and subjected to increased focus, once they had emerged. Smith and Geoffrey represented a collaboration between insider participant and outsider ethnographer. In Britain, more orthodox sociological studies of schools were taking place, using a mix of statistical and structured participant observation, (Hargreaves, 1967; Lacey, 1970). These and later studies by Woods (1979) and Ball (1981) were not driven by theories of empowerment but maintained the mainstream ethnographic tradition of immersion in a culture and the depiction and analysis of it for a largely academic audience. The problematics of actors' understandings of the momentarily entwined nature of their lives with those of the researcher were not part of the process. In this respect the research can be seen to be summative and judgmental. Despite the orthodox attempts by these researchers to 'dematerialize' in the role of fellow teacher, high profile observer or wall fly, the mechanics of such research remain firmly in the closed fist of the ethnographer.

For this researcher, such approaches are outdated and lead to further academic imperialism in education and elsewhere. Following in the tradition of Smith and Geoffrey, much of the research studies which have led to insights recorded in this book, I have undertaken in the spirit of collaboration (Sanger, 1990). They cover the last ten years. The 'liberation theology' of Freire (1977) and others still shapes research, today, but, probably, also undercut by the newer critiques and theoretical structures, loosely banded together under the term, 'postmodernism'. Much of the debate in this book, hinges on these developments, whether feminist, post-structuralist, action research in orientation or emanating from diverse disciplines such as literary theory, psychoanalysis or education.

The post-modern enterprise may suggest that:

> There is no foundational narrative. All human ideas are situated. Thus there is no neutral, universal reason available as an arbiter of truth and knowledge. Similarly, there is no empirical, knowable object called the 'self', waiting to be discovered or observed. The 'self' is best understood as a subjectivity produced within the discourses in which it is positioned and positions itself. (Griffiths, 1995)

17

In the chapters that follow, some of the major issues in doing observations against this backdrop of competing schools of research and evolving philosophical positions, will be revisited. The emphasis will be upon practicability and impact for change. I will attempt to refine my position on the historical map of evolving traditions, to which I alluded, earlier in this chapter. Nevertheless, the focus will be on doing observation in research. I hope that what ensues will be useful to other researchers even though they might position themselves at different cartographic points.

3 'Inside Out or Outside In?'

Expectation plays an ambiguous role in the process of observation. In evaluative research, for example, it is a useful tool in setting up an analytical model. How do professionals create targets, rhetoric, aims and objectives about their practice? Observation, it is assumed, can then confirm that these expectations are being met or otherwise. On the other hand, such expectations may lead, as with Nazruddin and the Donkey or Avebury, to blindness in the face of the obvious. Both researcher and participant may be operating under false assumptions and understandings.

Roland Barthes in *Camera Lucida* (1982), embarks on a quest to determine the artistic merits of photography. His professed wish was to:

> . . . learn at all costs what Photography was 'in itself', by what essential features it was to be distinguished from the community of images.
> (p. 3)

His investigations led him to differentiate photography into the field of study (studium), of which all photographs are a part, and those individual photographs in which some element (punctum) punctures the blandness of this field. In many ways this parallels the problem for observation, generally. For the teacher, the classroom is so familiar it can become a part of the bland field of study. For the nurse, the ward may be over-familiar and for the policeman, the canteen a wood of identical trees. Barthes' choice of individual photographs which puncture reality or rip the fabric of daily life, are highly subjective. They are chosen because they destabilize **his** unwitting immersion in the culture of photography. He infers, too, that the work of disciplines such as social science, as they seek to describe the world, are attracted to the phenomenological essence of the particular, and then, in their descriptions, they mortify it.

This leads, him to a hypothetical beginning to his research which is familiar to those researchers who would 'case study' individual classrooms, words, platoons or factory units.

> So I resolved to start my enquiry with no more than a few photographs, the ones I was sure existed for *me*. Nothing to do with a corpus: only some bodies. In this (after all) conventional debate between science and subjectivity, I had arrived at this curious notion;

why mightn't there be somehow, a new science for each object? A
mathesis singularis (and no longer *universalis?*'). (p. 8)

It seems that here there might be a good starting point for the researcher who
wants to observe with a different vision than that clouded by every day familiarity. Rather than observing people and objects as samples of larger groups in
some presupposed classificatory system such as the common one for example,
used to denote teaching style — didactic, child-centred, resource-based etc —
examine them in their complex singularity. Build up the range of observations,
seek those characteristics which are shared by them and thence evolve a
classification from the data. This may be the only way we can test implicit and
explicit systems of differentiation, handed down to us via cultural assumption.
Whilst doing so we must be aware of the dangers of seeking to develop
classification systems in the first place. Foucault (1989) is very expansive in
this regard, suggesting that the very act of classifying usually implies a dominance of rationalism and linearity over subjective and parallel experiences. His
word for it is *logocentric* behaviour.

For Barthes this meant locating the reasons why an individual photograph
arrested his attention, why his seeing became observation. A typical example
is in the Kertesz image (p. 82), called *Ernest* (*Paris, 1931*) which shows a boy,
in shorts, by his school desk. Coats are hung up on the wall behind. One
elbow rests in rather adult fashion on his desk. There is a knowing in his eyes
which embraces trhe photographer and, therefore, the viewer. A solitary other
pupil sits behind him. She seems as much an audience as anyone looking at
the photograph. All of which makes Barthes think about the 'inexorable ex-
tinction of the generations'.

A dialogue which leads, inevitably, to his own mortality. For those of us
concerned with breaking free from that which blinkers our observation, we
may need a similar arrest to our attention, something which leads us into a
more meditative engagement with what we observe. In the following extract,
Maxine Wood, a middle school teacher sees herself on video-tape. Suddenly
she realizes her role in a tableau vivant:

> The video made of my class by Charles Hull showed that very often
> when a child brought me a book with written work in, I would take
> it from the child and retain physical control over it. The ownership of
> the work was thus transferred to me . . . I prefer now to look at the
> work together while the child holds the book, . . . (Wood, 1989, p. 82)

Here, the punctum is the sudden observation of the image of the self, acting
in an everyday way, but arrested by self-perception and charged with a meaning she had not assigned to that kind of act before. An act that had been
repeated how many thousands of times in her teaching history?

This is essentially an inductive approach to observation. It means that

'It is possible that Ernest is still alive today: but where? how? What a novel!'

observation becomes a tool by which understanding is developed from the field of study. An alternative use for observation in research is to impose upon the field a framework which guides observation. Quantificatory research relies upon such frameworks. By classifying the kinds of items the observer wishes to capture on a check list, for example, before entering the social world, the observer is able to accumulate evidence by ticking the list whenever these sought-after behaviours occur (see chapter 5).

A way to explain the difference in these approaches, both of which are perfectly acceptable within their contexts, is to try to solve the following observation dilemma,

21

> How would we observe football hooligans at a match and report on their behavioural patterns?

An approach which uses prior classification would ensure we know how to recognize hooligans from their likely appearances, and then we could watch out for them and note what they get up to. At one time this would involve a classificatory system including tee shirts with ripped sleeves, even in mid-winter, close-cropped hair, Levis, Doc Martens, etc, etc. But this popular image underwent a punctum-like jolt when the police used closed circuit cameras and discovered that sometimes the main progenitors of violence at matches were young professional men in designer clothes. In order for the observer to have discovered this, the stereotypical description would have had to be excised from the mind. Classification of 'hooligan types' would need to follow open- ended observations within stadia. In my own experience, with this goal (!) in view, I would have had, using the criteria of **violence and disruption** rather than **appearance** to guide my open ended observations, an interesting range of data. By the end of my research *I would have included policemen, football stewards, players and a whole new range of spectators* within my developing observational embrace!

By this circuitous route we come to the nub of the cryptic chapter heading. *Inside out or outside in?* We deal with the issue in more detail in the next chapter when we look at the ethics of observation. However, we have to decide now which broad style of observation is most suited to a particular task. As with the observational problem of football hooliganism, decisions made at the outset of observation seriously can influence research findings at the other end of the process.

An Equinox programme (ITV, December 1991) examined the latest research into rheumatoid arthritis. A section of the programme showed how, whilst previous research into cell malfunction had concentrated upon proteins within the cells, the latest and very promising line of enquiry was examining the, until now neglected, sugar coating on the outside of cells.

Observations, therefore, can be made, as Barthes might have it, by looking at the collected evidence and seeking to discriminate the significant from the insignificant within that evidence. Or, decisions about significance may be made before observation takes place and thus the evidence is selected rather than collected. It is an intriguing debate, which is blurred by those who profess to do inductive research and yet conduct their observations against a research agenda, operating hypothetico-deductively within an inductive framework.

It would be ludicrous to suggest that we can go into the research site and blank our minds from the discordant clamour of research hypotheses, but with training and experience it is possible to still these demanding voices and focus in closely, or open the lens to a wider angle. The problem of the observer missing the significant tends to grow, the wider the attempted lens angle. The reason is straightforward enough. The more we try to take in, the greater the variety of signals reaching our minds and the more we have to be selective to make sense of them. Whether it is true that the human brain can take and sort up to seven channels of information at once is not that significant to social observation. The foci of observational work is not of the seven-separate-planes-arriving-at-an-airport, type, but rather an implicated skein of coloured threads wrapped round each other, creating harmonies, dissonances, frissons, blending and contrasting, and each one humming with a different sound! It is no wonder that the observer would prefer to focus on, say, red in middle C.

What can we achieve with training? Certainly a widening of the lens. Possibly a state of passive engagement, where images, sounds and smells are allowed to deluge the brain and a kind of inductive interpretation takes place.

> Yet, at the heart of psychopathology lies a fundamental confusion between the self as object and the self of pure subjectivity. Emotions, thoughts, impulses, images and sensations are the contents of our consciousness: we witness them; we are aware of their existence. Likewise, the body, the self-image, and the self-concept are all constructs that we observe. But our core sense of personal existence — the 'I' — is located in awareness itself, not in its content. (Deikman, 1982, p. 10)

There are connections here with Herrigel's (1972) account of learning archery under the Zen Master. He talks of the target shooting the arrow, drawing it into itself, of its symbolism in a spiritual sense:

> And consequently, by the 'art' of archery he does not mean the ability of the sportsman, which can be controlled, more or less, by bodily exercises, but an ability whose origin is to be sought in spiritual exercises and whose aim consists in hitting a spiritual goal, so that fundamentally the marksman aims at himself and may even succeed in hitting himself. (p. 14)

A state of mind can be achieved which enables the observer to be more receptive to what is happening outside pure awareness: to be less obviously selective of data and to have a more naive engagement with the milieu under study. Equally, a state of mind can be achieved which forecloses on all data that is regarded as superfluous to what is deemed to be significant. Perhaps a useful dichotomy is one which promotes the unstructured observational strategy in the early period of a research project, whilst the more focussed approach comes into its own later, as the researcher becomes convinced of the significances within the enquiry.

In both instances, as well as at all the stages between these polar positions, observation seems to work best if the observer is calm, feels unthreatened and at ease with the role. Various tricks of the trade in observation are dealt with in the next chapter but suffice it to say, at this point, that an observer who is ill at ease, communicates this to those under observation. State of mind is important. It is aided by a fervent belief in the importance of the events to which the observer is witness.

The constraints upon the novice researcher have already been foreshadowed. Classrooms, wards, canteens or shop floors open and close to perception, sometimes appearing translucent and at others opaque. Teachers, pupils, nurses, patients or police personnel become mercurial variables. Easy explanations are regarded with suspicion. Nothing must be as it seems. Very soon it appears that nothing is as it was. There are no constants to act as anchors or ground against which people's actions can be plotted. Events appear more and more singular or idiosyncratic. Causalities fray and tear and are carried away by time. Entering the field with the inheritance of theory often leads to the feeling of being inadequately or over-dressed for an important event. Adrift and sometimes with reception jammed by the sheer volume of noise all round. For many, ethnography can signal drowning rather than waving.

I recall researching in sites in London, over a hundred miles from my research base, a sort of immersus interruptus. Imagine Malinovski returning every three days for fresh provisions.

What occurred in those early days was a sort of mutation of what I believed fieldwork to be. There were observations, interviews, casual conversations, documentation and analyses, some of which was negotiated, some not. I found myself being opportunistic because I might have to leave soon. I began deliberately to overhear what people were saying. I would find myself following a digression of great interest but little apparent relevance to my research. How did I allow the slippage to occur? At times my approach leant towards the ethnomethodological, as when staff explained their diaries of project work or their timetables. At times it seemed more ethnological, particularly at moments of reimmersion after a longish lay-off and when the staff seemed to have forgotten my existence. There were even moments of what Eisner (1972) has termed 'connoisseurship' as in drama lessons, when class and teacher appeared pat of a total drama played out for the private appreciation of this audience of one. Non-participation occasionally lurched into participation.

Some of my fellow students then, and those I have supervised later, were even worse off. At least I was collecting data and there was some comfort in the initial piles of interview tapes and observation notebooks. For some, there seemed little difference between one set of data and the next. They couldn't establish the nature of significance in their study. Fear of the field became a palpable anxiety.

How can this process of entering the field of study be made easier? How can the novice researcher engage with meaningful observation at the earliest possible opportunity?

The Key to Entry

The following diagram was one I developed for an Open University Curriculum Planning course. The logic of it is to see in the mind's eye, the process with

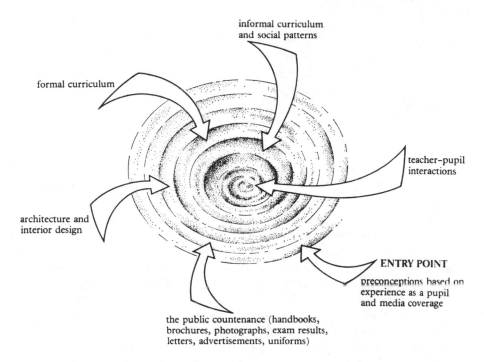

informal curriculum
and social patterns

formal curriculum

teacher–pupil
interactions

architecture and
interior design

ENTRY POINT

preconceptions based on
experience as a pupil
and media coverage

the public countenance (handbooks,
brochures, photographs, exam results,
letters, advertisements, uniforms)

which you will observe-your-way-in to the core of the research study. From the moment you start negotiating or deliberating entry to the site(s), every detail of the route in, may turn out to have significance. When access must be negotiated, as usually happens in most research into people's working lives, there is rich information available from the outset. Some of this will be documentation, some of it architecture and furnishings, some will be curriculum or working patterns and some will be the baggage of preconceptions which we carry around with us anyway.

There are two schools of thought (at least) about how much you front-load your attitudes and expectations before going into the field. There are those who only feel secure in knowing as much about the people and issues as is possible. This can have its obvious consequences in prejudicing perception. On the other hand, you can gain credibility for having the expertise. Knowing so much can help the development of unconscious theorising which can lead to bias in your perceptions of the field. Alternatively, if your stay is to be short, foreknowledge might be the only way you have of trying to determine what you are seeing, and asking pertinent questions. The longer the possible stay at the research site, the less the researcher needs to swot up. S/he can keep an open mind and develop a sense of people and issues through a gradual accretion of knowledge based on how the social actors, themselves, are constructing them. It depends on the kind of research that is being attempted as to whether the issues are tightly drawn at the outset, as they may be in some evaluative research, or whether the issues are themselves part of the research findings, as they would be if, for example, the brief was to discover why a school, police force or business was under-achieving.

Whilst it would be trite to suggest that researchers empty their minds before going off into the field, there is much to be said for self-examination at the outset, of one's knowledge, attitudes and prejudices. For some this can act as a necessary brake on the inclination towards unconscious bias, once they arrive on site. Write preconceptions down in the field notebook. At the very least they can take the form of hypotheses that have to be tested, rather than potential pools of contamination.

Research designs which are based on hypotheses testing suit the individual who finds it difficult to cope with all the ambiguities of open-ended tasks.

Personal Preparation

Make sure you are ready for all contingencies. Notebooks laid out in the style you feel suits the circumstances. Plenty of pens and pencils. Camera loaded and fully charged. Tape recorder or camcorder primed with your full, practised knowledge of how to use them (see chapter 7).

Are you dressed so that you blend, rather than clash with your research surroundings? Would particular changes in the way you are presenting yourself help with authority figures, middle managers, recidivists, pupils . . .

Have you agreed a time of arrival and someone who will meet you, so that you are not treated with suspicion by all and sundry. Or is it better to arrive early and wander about, gauging the ethos, checking notice boards and overhearing what people say, before they know who you are. The research setting should determine this.

Always have an account ready of what you are there for, what your principles of procedure are (chapter 4), and a non-specific, non-judgmental summary of what you, yourself believe. The less you give away about what you know or expect to find out, the better. Many people you meet as a researcher need to be educated about research approaches. Apart from talking about the research process, talk little and observe closely. Get used to writing things down rather than saving them up for later. It feels strange at first, particularly with people about, but you should stick to it and try to be unostentatious about it. Always write down insights, explanations or interpretations. Keep them separate from your factual accounts.

Postscript

Take the following story:

A man observes his dog throwing the white rabbit pet of the children next door, up in the air and catching it, he races outside to find it muddy, bloody and dead. Thinking quickly he takes it into the house, washes it, dries it with a hair drier and puts it back in its hutch. He meets the father of the children later that evening. His neighbour is agitated; 'Do you know, the kids' rabbit died this morning and I buried it. When I came back from work the bugger was back in its hutch!'

Why do we find it funny? Presumably because we are aware that appearances may be deceptive, that observation needs the back up of further evidence and that, given the circumstances, our minds can run away with theories for what is happening based on what seems, at first contact, incontrovertible evidence.

Now was the dog owner here, inside or outside the event? Or both? In the following account, the same problem arises for the observer. When a new headteacher told this story of the nature of evidence and consequent decision making, the participants in the workshop did not stop laughing for minutes on end.

I spent the Easter holidays looking round my new school, I wanted to create a good impression with staff. A new start after years of atrophy. I though that there were two things that I could do before they returned after the Easter vacation. I would replace the dilapidated furniture in the staffroom and I would do something about the pigeons which were nesting in the cloakroom and defecating on the children's' clothes! The first was easy. I bought some nice comfortable chairs and a carpet from an auction and burned the old. The pigeons were more of a problem. Eventually, the Health Inspector said they must be shot as they would come in with the children every morning. This was done. On the first morning of the new term I had two deputations. One from parents and one from staff. The parents were upset because the two school pigeons, Elsie and George, reared from young by the children, had 'disappeared'. The staff were upset because the chairs, brought from their own homes, and with high sentimental value, seemed to have been spirited away! (In the interests of anonymity, the pigeons' names have been changed in this account.)

To be outside (etic) can mean not understanding the order of significance people place upon objects, persons and events in their culture or sub-culture. To be inside (emic) may provide the observer with the role of cultural agent and the capacity to inform those on the outside. May. It can backfire, too! Remember the seminal anthropological texts, centred on Samoa and authored by Margaret Mead? Later, the work was possibly discredited by the Samoans, themselves, who may have indicated that they had deliberately hoodwinked the anthropologist during her long stay with them. Then again. . . .

4   The Ethics of Entry

Imagine that, in the normal run of things, you are sitting at work in your professional setting, in front of your class of students, or the committee of which you are chair or the colleague whom you and the panel are interviewing. As you become involved in the proceedings, with its explicit or implicit agenda, you find yourself distracted by the regular and somewhat penetrative gaze of an individual to whom you have not been introduced. What is more, she appears to have a tape recorder running and is making notes. What questions cross your mind? Maybe some or all of the following — and others:

> 'Who is she?'
> 'Who gave her permission to be here?'
> 'What have I been saying, for God's sake?'
> 'Who is she working for?'
> 'What is she making of all this?'
> 'What's a fly on the wall like her doing in a place like this?'

As the hot flushes of indignation, guilt, fear or anger stir up the emotions, what do you do? Face her angrily? She may be there by agreement with a superior. Hurriedly curtail the proceedings? That might reflect badly on your professionalism. Continue as before? But you thought the proceedings were private and confidential. You are caught. Maybe, in the circumstances, you find yourself unable to perform satisfactorily. You lose the thread of your argument. You stammer. And so on.

This is not as outlandish a vignette as might be supposed. As a researcher I have frequently found myself in circumstances where people have not been informed of my impending or actual presence. Particularly in schools, hospitals or the police force where the hierarchical system produces staff who have such an ingrained belief in their own authority and the subordination of colleagues to that authority. A quick explanation would give everyone the chance to prepare for my invasion of their lives. Instead, I had to introduce myself, my work, my ethical base and my methods to each individual with whom I came into contact, whether child or adult. There have been occasions, for example in London in the mid-1980s, where it has taken me time to appreciate that even an explanation is not enough. Trying to elicit the views of young skinheads required going much further. Reducing hair length considerably and wearing jeans helped, but effecting an introduction via one of the group was the key.

This geezer's a researcher. He's OK.

The problem the observer faces in his/her role is that by merely being there, he/she highlights for everyone the political nature of both working and social life.

The handful of questions, asked at the beginning of this chapter about the female stranger, only underline the concerns that people feel, even when they are informed as to why the observer is going to be present. So there remains the question of how access to events and people is negotiated. And does such a negotiation afford better data or hamper enquiries? When is it better to be covert and when is it better to be overt?

In most circumstances it would be wise to go to extremes in negotiating an observational presence. Given that people are concerned, rightly, that what you might reveal are their failings and consequently you may be losing them their jobs or terminating a project, unit of operations or funding, the tighter the negotiation the more they tolerate your presence. Below is a typical set of procedures I have developed with teachers in classrooms. The way the procedures were developed can be found in chapter 9. For all practitioners, their traditional autonomy within the workplace is threatened by observation. They know that it is difficult ever to achieve all their goals when working with other human beings. They know that observations may reveal failings. They know that one lesson, one ward shift, one case of arrest for a driving misdemeanour is never quite like another: that children, patients and passers by are volatile variables, one day grasping the meaning of events and the next day seemingly stubbornly unwilling to accept them at face value. They know that their instinctive handling of aspects of their professional work may be severely affected by the presence of a stranger. They know that their own emotional circumstances, that of a disruptive child, transgressor, patient, their health, their morale or the surrounding culture of other professionals can all inhibit what they are trying to do. In such circumstances, what ethical procedures would seem to offer fairness, relevance and accuracy in doing observation?

The following example was devised in order to support staff development, that is, to help improve professionals in their work.

Principles of Procedures in Workplace Observation

All activities involving workplace observation should be deemed confidential unless otherwise negotiated. The major responsibility for these activities and control over their consequences lies with the practitioner in the work place. The observation activity should be practitioner-led and not observer-led.

Workplace observation requires negotiation between practitioner and observer to:-

• define and refine the focus of observation against a frank communication of the working context
• explore the methodology to be used in the observation to collect data
• establish observer presence, behaviour and status in the workplace
• plan a feedback session soon after the observation

The practitioner 'owns' any material products of an observation and may destroy them if necessary (notes, audio-tapes, video tapes, check lists).

The observation should be arranged in an optimistic climate of professional trust, in the belief that it will improve knowledge about the work of professional staff.

Here, there is clear intent that observation is conducted via protocols which minimize the possible damage to the professional who is being observed. The whole accent of these protocols is on the autonomy of the practitioner and enables the individual to develop his/her own agenda for professional development and change. What happens when the purpose is not staff development but, rather, research or an evaluation enquiry? Would the principles need altering?

In the following extract from the protocols of an early evaluation project, on which I collaborated (Norris and Sanger, 1984) one can clearly see the shift from upholding the autonomy of respondents, to a position of a more guarded, (self-interested) respect for participants.

Confidentiality

1 No interview or observational data, meetings, verbal or written exchanges will be considered as 'off the record', but those involved will have opportunities to correct or improve statements, and in some instances to withdraw or restrict the dissemination of statements.
2 Attributed, or readily identifiable quotations, perspectives or judgments will not be published without the approval of those to whom they are attributed or with whom they may be readily identified.
3 Correspondingly, information related to individual or institutional experience which is effectively anonymized or generalized, may be reported without specific clearance from the individual or institutional source.
4 The evaluation team accepts that the validity of the accounts it produces depends critically upon participant endorsement; between data gathering and reporting the evaluators will take every opportunity to check the accuracy, fairness and relevance of their accounts with those whose work they represent.
5 These principles of confidentiality and procedures for negotiation cannot be invoked to suppress evaluation reports or to exclude from consideration activities or issues of importance in the presentation of the Project experience.

Access to Data and Its Release

1 The evaluation will seek only reasonable access to the work and personnel of the project or institutions.
2 Respondents will be given the opportunity to comment on the fairness, accuracy and relevance of reports concerning them and opportunities will be sought if necessary and possible to improve reports in respect of these comments. In some instances the team could be unwilling to change the report: if this should arise, the report will contain whatever additional commentary those concerned wish to attach to it. Dissemination of evaluation reports will be phased to allow effective opportunities for their improvement through consultation.

The politics of independent evaluation are to be clearly seen here. The in-built defiance of powerful interest groups and the certainties of the trade. For example, methodological issues are not negotiable, nor is there any nod in the direction of the ambiguity, not to mention arbitrariness of knowledge. Whilst relying heavily upon MacDonald's (1977) inspirational democratic evaluation to give the protocols shape, there is a toughness about the bargaining posture.

In many ways, Wittgenstein (1953) would be happy with the language game and form of life evidenced here. The setting up of rules, which explicitly state power relations at the outset, seem, on the surface exemplary. But Wittgenstein would ask serious questions about whether such a manifesto of intent was sufficiently understood by all actors, for the protocols to have anything more than symbolic meaning.

The notion of 'off the record', for example. Nothing in the evaluation can be regarded as off the record. Everything is 'on the record'. However, most of us would balk at writing that in our protocols. It implies a comprehensiveness that we know we can't attain. Nothing is 'off the record' allows us a certain conceit, which neatly covers our deceit. It allows us to select significance from the deluge of data with all its ambiguities and uncertainties and pretend that we have weighed up and rejected the rest. A post-structuralist critique of such a notion would suggest that the protocols are an attempted vehicle for drawing up a narrative with no margins, no omissions, where the text literally fills up the entire page. The grand narrative which allows no alternatives. The fact that respondents are persuaded that they can act to improve such a narrative is merely a cooption to the enterprise by implying that there is only one, overriding story to be told. And this story is the one that the evaluator constructs out of the mouths of others and through their eyes. The appeal, later in the protocols, that accuracy, fairness and relevance underpin the evaluator/evaluatee relationship similarly disguise an authoritarian intent. There is a perfect illustration of this in Rouse (1994), who deliberates on the following lines from Foucault:

> There can be no such thing as a truth independent of its regime, unless it be that of another. So that liberation in the name of 'truth' could only be a substitution of another system of power for this one. (p. 104)

In protocols 2 and 3 there is, effectively, a further demonstration of power at the expense of the subjects of evaluation. The anonymization of accounts and/ or the generalization of experience has a strong flavour of rewriting history, against explicit or implicit criteria. Effacing individuals' experience and viewpoints has a totalitarian ring to it.

When we move on to the second, procedural area of the protocols, we have terms such as 'reasonable', a repeat of 'fairness', 'accuracy' and 'relevance', together with the acceptance of the right to a participant's minority export should the event merit it.

The invocation of the observer/researcher in social settings, as a fully actualized Maslovian individual, is inescapable. It is a hard act to live up to. One is left feeling that agreeing to such protocols is rather like signing a contract when you buy goods; the kind of contract which actually signs away your rights. The participants may be in a far stronger position in **not** accepting the protocols and relying upon more subtle means of interacting with these outsiders to their kingdoms.

So, in the name of negotiation, what are we left with? Do we head down the road of reflecting our concern for participants' understandings, as the prima mobile of validity, or do we invoke special status, calling upon our interpretative resources as social agents, specialists in particular disciplines and players within the language games in question. The former hands-on responsibility for interpretation to participants while the latter keeps that role in the hands of the researcher or evaluator. At some point in whichever position we take, we will have to involve the other because our evidence is always going to represent participant understandings and meaning-making — and, therefore, the politics of information exchange. The kind of protocols we have been examining may be the nearest we can get to a formal contract of evaluation relationship, if we see evaluation as a form of contracted information extraction from the mouths of the willing and the unwilling.

Research, as opposed to evaluation, as has often been pointed out, is not, on the surface, as likely to be injurious to the health of respondents. The parameters are usually broader and the outcomes are not usually so tied in to recommendatory findings. This is not to say that respondents need no protection. On the contrary. Here, the likelihood of harm is more likely to be related to exposure to public scrutiny than the professional scrutiny manifest in most evaluation. Also, researchers enter the dynamics of social relations, with all their checks and balances, and by asking questions, often make these social relations and activities questionable to those engaged in them. In Canada I was intrigued to find that the ethics of classroom research involved showing that the research would not prejudice the chances of children **not** engaged in the study, as well as those engaged in it.

The process of negotiation always involves either developing trust, or developing explicit, written guarantees. For example, here is a letter that we have sent to parents on a current project at The Centre for Applied Research in Management, Education and Training.

Apart from this being a letter of intent, generally descriptive of the project's purpose and methods, it merely seeks cooperation. There are no promises other than the suggestion that it is going to help education in some indefinable way. And the parents can always back out.

Gaining cooperation is harder to achieve in these days of media abuse of trust. Whereas, as we have seen, the whole business of writing protocols is subject to easy torpedoing. At the end of this process, someone, researcher or evaluator, must enter the *mise en scene* carrying documentation of proof of identity and role, as though in a high security area. The alternatives are to do covert research, or proxy research.

Dear

I am writing to ask you and your family for help with a research study currently being undertaken by a research team based at City College, Norwich. This exciting project has the backing of the British Film Institute and the British Library.

We are interested in investigating the possible effects of various entertainment media (for example, video and computers) on young children's thinking and understanding. As part of our study, we are hoping to observe and interview 100 young children (4–9 years) drawn from schools in and around Norwich. This will provide us with valuable information about the ways in which children are currently using media equipment and how they are applying the skills acquired through these activities.

In order to obtain as much information as possible, we need to observe the children both at home and at school.

The headteacher and staff at your school believe that this is a worthwhile study that will provide useful information about future teaching and learning. They are happy to cooperate with the research based in the school and will assist us as much as they can.

All children selected for inclusion in the project will be observed and interviewed in the school setting by one of the researchers over a period of a few days. One member of the research team will then visit the child at home and watch him/her playing. This will also be an opportunity to talk to parents and other members of the family about their attitudes to video, TV and computers.

The research findings from this high-profile project are likely to have nationwide importance. The project team consists of a small group of experienced researchers and teachers who will endeavour to conduct the study with as little intrusion as possible and with respect for your privacy and confidentiality. No information will be released which identifies your child without your permission and you will have the right to withdraw from the research project at any time.

We hope that you will allow your child to participate in this exciting project and we would appreciate it if you would complete the tear-off slip at the bottom of the letter and return it to your child's school as soon as possible. A member of the research team will then contact you to arrange a mutually convenient time to visit you at home.

If you would like any more information about the project, please contact the headteacher, who will be able to supply more details or, if you prefer, put you in touch with a member of the research team.

Yours sincerely

Professor Jack Sanger

Reply slip

I agree that my child..can participate in the entertainment media project.

I understand that I can withdraw my child from the project at any time.

Signature of parent/guardian ....

Covert Research

I can't say I am over-experienced at being a researcher among the unwitting. There are occasions where I have glimpsed the potential of being covert: behind a video camera pointed at a playground, for instance, or behind a closed circuit tv set-up at a football stadium. I recall an early example of entrapment when a colleague tape-recorded someone's words in order to hang them in a later enquiry. Despite feeling that the victim of this subterfuge was guilty of extraordinarily unprofessional and harmful practice, it still seemed morally indefensible to be talking together, knowing that the recorder was turning silently round, concealed in a bag by our feet. At one point I recorded (despite claims that I wouldn't) senior staff in an organization, being racist. I also spent time among the worst offenders in football crowds, with my tape running unseen, picking up the prairie fire progress of new football chants. At other times, covert research does not seem so bad. For example, pretending to be a customer at a store, to try to elicit attitudes of staff, or seeking information at a tourist office or library to test the capacity of staff to provide useful information. This role-based participant observation would seem to be one of our rights within a community — although how we use the information may transgress the ethical.

The sort of covert activity to be found in investigative journalism, private detective agencies and in-house information gathering in organizations is not usually found within funded research and evaluation, although individuals pursuing postgraduate qualifications, with topic areas such as race, gender, drugs, prostitution, pederasty and so on, may opt for covert strategies. But the dangers do not need expanding on here.

There are arguments for covert observation which stem from concerns about the Hawthorne Effect. People are affected by the researcher's presence and don't act naturally. Become covert and catch them doing what they normally do. Like sitting in a hide, watching the wild fowl. Two way mirrors in laboratories have their place, perhaps. Whether there is any great distortion in the researcher proclaiming his or her role and presence, is debatable. Much of it depends upon context. Who has what to lose? If the desired goal is an illumination of context, then the loss may be so minimal that the researcher is tolerated. If people might lose their jobs, don't expect neutrality and openness.

Gamekeeper Turning Poacher

Even when everyone knows who you are and why you are there, there are certain tricks of the trade which enable you to become relatively covert in a variety of settings. They are simple and easily mastered. Basically they boil down to being a chameleon:

- Wear appropriate clothing (colour match, style) to the context.
- Try not to make eye contact.
- Trawl with the eyes rather than focus on one place, sweeping over your subject at intervals.
- Emulate the norm with your body position (sitting, standing).
- Emulate the norm in the activity being observed (reading, writing etc.).
- Say little and show just a mild interest in proceedings.
- Choose a position to observe which allows you most scope but does not identify you with a role (for example, sitting at the front of a class identifies you with the teacher).
- Enter the scene of observation with the participants, as much as possible. Late or early arrival accentuates your outsider status.
- Have your presence explained beforehand.

As researchers we are always walking the fine line of how much people should know about our activities and how unobtrusive we can be, in order to gather 'authentic' data. To do research, therefore, confers upon the researcher the responsibility *to act ethically for the other*. What this means is that the researcher, given his/her privileged status and knowledge of the consequences of research activities, must protect, as well as possible, participants who are unaware of the consequences research and evaluation may have for them.

Proxy Observation

Research projects are carried out utilizing whole cohorts of observers, operating within their own milieux. Mass observation research involving representative individuals in all walks of life, is conducted via their diaries or log books. Since these individuals have none of the problems of blending into their everyday settings, They have access to data that outsiders find it more difficult to gather. They can also inscribe their own feelings, thoughts, insights and prejudices alongside the data. These 'moles' can be particularly effective, in the action research paradigm.

Action research takes many forms. At its heart is the rubric that the practitioner is best placed to research his or her own practice as a means to understanding and improving that practice. I have written elsewhere and often enough, how action research can become dominated by the imperialistic interests of academia, most recently (Sanger, 1995c). Ideally, action research is conducted by practitioners without the help of external facilitators. But the cooption of practitioners for the benefits of research projects and programmes represents the norm. here, the action research is driven by project aims and objectives and the work is facilitated by the researcher breed.

With good negotiation and a researcher ideology of subordination to participant agendas and practical interests, an action research project can provide relatively large scale gathering of sensitive, subtle and complex data, which the outside researcher would find it difficult to gather.

In a current research project at CARMET, investigating the sexual health education of people with learning difficulties, a group of practitioners from all the relevant care areas, is doing just that. Within a strict set of guidelines, overseen by a medical ethics committee, they are investigating individual life histories, their own and their colleagues' professional practices and the delivery of sexual health education within their institutions. What they are uncovering would be impossible to generate by survey or outsider researcher coming into the milieu. Here are minutes from a recent action research, critical group gathering, only first names of action researchers are given. Clients' names are indicated by letter, only:

1 Understanding Concepts

Sharon illustrated with her case study, -D——, that some individuals have a need for a very black and white image of what is presented to them. Client D——, for example, visualized the body as a tank which fills up with food, and menstruation as a broken egg inside the body.

2 Sex as Function of Procreation

Examples were offered by Sharon and Edward of clients who believed sexual intercourse only took place and only needed to take place when a couple decided to have children.

5 Abuse is not Sexual

Gorete mentioned that some clients have difficulty in recognizing some situations that they have been in as sexual; she illustrated this with the story of a client who did not report a violent rape, because that was the way that she had always experienced sex.

Postscript

I am grateful to Docker (1994) for the following quotation from Apuleius (1980):

The dreadful condition of these poor beasts, whom, I might soon be brought to resemble, so depressed me that I drooped my head like them and grieved for the degradation into which I had fallen since those far off days when I was Lord Lucius. My only consolation was the unique opportunity I had of observing all that was said and done around me; because nobody showed any reserve in my presence. Homer was quite right to characterise Odysseus, whom he offered as an example of the highest wisdom and prudence, as one who 'visited many cities and come to know many different peoples'. I am grateful now whenever I recall those days: my many adventures in ass-disguise enormously enlarged my experience, even if they have not taught me wisdom. It was at this mill that I picked up a story which I hope will amuse you as much as it amused me. (p. 180)

5 Validity and Invalidity Benefits

Truth is never pure, and rarely simple
(Oscar Wilde, *The Importance of Being Ernest*, Act 1)

When people say that trials are objective and impartial means of producing legal judgments, what they really mean is that trials rely on a
standardized means of packaging and analyzing information: the story.
The reconstruction of evidence in the form of a story does not guarantee that the truth will emerge in a trial, nor does it ensure that all
the possible interpretations of evidence will be considered. Storytell-
ing simply provides defendants with a means of reconstructing an
incident to their best advantage and presenting the reconstruction to
an audience who will judge it according to its plausibility. In principle,
this feature of trials ought to provide a universal safeguard against
false or misguided accusation and conviction. In fact, however, this
protection of the justice process only holds if all parties in an adjudi-
cation have the same capacity to present and judge stories. (Bennett
and Feldman, 1981, p. 171)

We will watch the lady being sawn in half because we know that she isn't.
Why is the event such a crowd puller even today, when technology produces
so many more complex, mind-bending miracles? Isn't it because we love experiencing, first hand, the sensation of our eyes deceiving us? The conflict
between rationality and primary data. The palpability of it. It signifies what we
know; namely that appearances are deceptive and that each day, to a greater
or lesser extent, we are fooled by the look of something. Certainties, we learn,
at the level of daily experience, are usually more alloy than cast iron. However, the influence of positivistic science in the nineteenth and early twentieth
century upon language and thought is such, that daily we override the ambiguities and doubts of sensory experiences with a rationalistic mind-set which
affirms concepts such as truth, validity and objectivity. It is an ironic confirmation of Schutz's (1967) separation of science from the every day, referred to in
the first chapter. For there is little debate about which value system holds sway
in the politicking of social life. The key terms of positivism became, and still
are, the coinage of superior values in our meritocratic class system.

Let us look more closely at the concept of validity. The term has a very particular meaning in all forms of research. Essentially, it refers to the accuracy and defensibility of any aspect of the research process. The research processes, themselves, that is the active data gathering and analysis, are scrutinised for their **internal validity**. In other words, are the chosen research methods suited to the aim of illuminating a particular research issue, or solving a particular research or evaluation problem. The relationship between the research as a whole and its import for the world beyond the research, is scrutinized for its **external validity**. Thus, we can draw in notions of generalizability and prediction. What is suggested in this book is that we can draw heavily upon notions of contingency, in this regard. Causality is not something I would advise social scientists to try to vouchsafe. Defensible research processes, in particular paradigms, are described as robust, rigorous and generalizable. They are said to have a construct validity. However, research takes many forms and these criteria may not be appropriate when it comes to some of them. Validity demands change as research becomes more applied, collaborative and designed to enable social actors to progress and learn from their histories. In these cases the criteria for validity may be different. Terms such as responsiveness, fairness, trustworthiness and accuracy may be used.

There is a spectrum of definitions as to what forms of proof engender validity. At the scientific method end of the spectrum, validity is confirmed through positivistic processes such as replication or the medical 'double blind' and at the other end it is confirmed by the invocation of more relativistic notions such as the 'shock of recognition' or 'thick description' or 'triangulation'. In the former, the expectation is that anyone coming after and reading what the researcher did, could repeat the research and achieve the same results. Or that succeeding researchers could try other approaches to disprove the research by developing new instruments. Or by widening the scope beyond the original research. Or by testing logical applications and consequences. Or by trying to find examples in the world which contradict the original findings (Popper, 1972). In the latter, analyses of the relationship between events and people achieve greater validity if participants who have been observed in the research, recognize themselves, their motives, their actions and their rationale in the researcher's recordings and reconstructions. Or those outside the research recognize that it echoes, in some confirmatory way, what they themselves feel to be right, or true or reliable, Or that the research achieves its analytic rigour by the initial comprehensiveness of its data collection techniques.

However, people being people, are not very reliable as subjects of attempts to achieve validity. They change their stories. They lie. They refuse to talk. They forget. They move on and become impossible to trace. They can have a lot to lose. It is accepted that the researcher may show that in certain uniform conditions, chemical reactions will always produce the same results. But who can say that of people? Would a group of individuals react even twice in the same way to the same set of circumstances? Is it possible to *have* the same set of circumstances? It's absurd. There are no real action replays in life.

And could you assemble an identical group to repeat the experiment? Not at all. Individuals and groups are as unique in their entirety as the finger prints they individually own. In a recent paper, I tried to explore this problem. It is the confusion over causality and contingency.

> David Hume demonstrated that causality as a guiding principle to human action, was in fact based on dubious premisses (Noxon, 1973). For example, people may well say that the nail went into the wood because it had been hammered. Hume suggested that the two events are not causally linked in this way. He showed that observation of the relationship merely indicates that the nail enters the wood following it being hammered. In strict terms, no-one can predict that events are caused by other events, merely that they may succeed them with regularity. There are so many circumstances surrounding even this simple act: the force of the blow, the accuracy, the strength of the nail, the quality of the hammer face, the condition and type of wood, the physical condition of the hammerer, gravity etc, etc. No matter how many times we witness successful hammering, we are still wrong in attributing causal relationships to hammer and nail. Such causal relations can only occur in a world of absolute uniformity. So what of events in the social world, where uniformity can only ever be a statistician's dream? When we talk of managers bringing about change or teachers introducing successful strategies into the classroom, where is our truth and where is our error? (Sanger, 1995b, pp. 93–105.)

That doesn't stop research into people, of course; their histories, their actions, their motivations and rationales. Chemicals may provide greater certainties but are they intrinsically as interesting? Chemicals may be predictable but people certainly are not. Who could, for example, have predicted the dismantling of the Berlin Wall and the collapse of the USSR, even a year before the events took place? Who can predict falling in love or what exact words are going to slip from his/her own lips next?

Research into human behaviour is notoriously fraught. Even in the laboratory, where every possible side issue or variable is controlled, subjects of experiments defy the certainties of hypothesis or theory, except in the most basic of experiments. Once out there in the world, the task would seem beyond control and achieving some reasonable meaning for human action, improbable. But this isn't the case. Why?

Why is it that we know that children will mostly learn to read and that some combination of the teaching methods we use will produce that effect? Or that if we allow a system to operate whereby hospital doctors work 100 hours a week, patient care deteriorates? Or that merely seeing cardboard cut-outs of police cars on our streets, reduces speeding?

It is because patterns for general human behaviour must be distinguished from expectations and predictions about particular individuals.

41

A parent tells a child to eat all that is in front of her. 'Think of all the starving children in Africa!', says the parent weightily. 'Tell me the name of just one of them', replies the child, crushingly.

Thus, validity in statistics relies upon research into the general rather than the particular. The higher the number of cases in the target population, the more such patterns will emerge and be found 'significant'. But this may only be of use at a general level. It may not help us in particular cases. To know that boys or girls are better than each other at certain subjects at certain ages, does not usually help a teacher with a particular class. To know that the lack of leisure facilities predisposes a young population to more crime, does not account for estates where, despite deprivation, crime levels are no more than anywhere else. Or, equally, high crime figures in pockets of the suburban well-to-do. Nor does the knowledge that patients usually die after a certain stage in cancer is reached, account for extraordinary recoveries in individuals. Individual human behaviour can not, and should not, be modelled on generalized findings.

We become aware, in research, that the levels of the general, and the particular, co-exist perfectly happily. They have different purposes. They are ways of seeing and understanding the world. And we create them. In that sense they are arbitrary. As long as we agree their purpose and function, they enable us to assure ourselves (or delude ourselves) that we are acting on evidence. Whereas the politician may want broad evidence for policy making to try to limit the spread of AIDS across huge populations, the individual sufferer may need a treatment plan, unique to him/her. For AIDS workers, case studies of sexual liaisons may provide better evidence with which to counsel the sexually active.

Attempts to integrate the two levels, general and particular, in ways which would allow us to forecast one from the other, have recently proven partially possible within chaos theory (Gleick, 1990). Complex turbulent systems such as weather, the stock exchange, epidemics, the death of stars or heart conditions are shown to be dependent on relatively basic, non-linear patterns of repeated occurrence. The slightest idiosyncrasies within these initial patterns could produce the huge system perturbations we encounter above our heads, in our bodies or with our stocks and shares. The metaphor commonly used for this condition has become an elegant cliché; the 'butterfly effect'. The beat of a butterfly's wings might sufficiently effect the immediately local air conditions to the effect that, eventually, it gives rise to the weather pattern, itself.

In some isomorphic way, there are parallels for researchers in social sciences. The study of the singular can give us understanding of aspects of the general. Through the cumulation of idiosyncratic evidence from individuals and groups, larger social patterns can be understood. For example, in research (Sanger, 1992) into how teenagers make decisions about whether to stay on at school or college, post-16, some 500 students' perceptions of the decision-making process were elicited, in a variety of settings. Their accounts, whether in groups or singly, on paper or through discussion, contained within them cumulative patterns. Thus, for example, **lethargy** appeared to be a factor in students going on to the sixth form of the school they had been attending previously. This kind of pattern was supported by observational evidence across a wide range of schools which showed that information was not made available in most schools to promote critical thought, explore alternatives and challenge students' apathy.

> What schools possibly don't realize is that the majority of students who stay on with them, may do so out of less than idealistic reasons. Students talked about:
>
> better the devil you know
> security of knowing your school well
> not being ready for the outside world
> keeping up friendships
> staying with teachers you know
> smaller and therefore friendlier
> continuing the tradition of brothers and sisters
> lethargy or inertia
>
> 'I stayed on at_____because I couldn't be bothered to go anywhere else. My friends were staying on here. I knew everything here.'
>
> (Sanger, 1991, p. 26)

The researchers into Staying On Rates were charged with trying to uncover decision-making patterns across a local authority but individual teachers would need to know the kinds of student decision-making that was occurring among individuals, too. Such evidence would inform their daily action, alert them to issues and note negative indicators in student behaviour. At the level required of it, the research seemed successful. It provided schools with a range of practices which ought to improve staying on rates, whilst endeavouring to take into account the quality of support for all students, including those who would be better served by leaving, even though they had qualified to stay on, at whatever institution they chose. But at other levels, the research made little inroads. Why did certain schools display sudden drops in their rates? Why did others suddenly increase their rates out of all proportion? What was the equivalent of the butterfly effect? A particular student deciding to stay on and affecting all his/her peers? A television programme? A new staff appointment? A crass statement made at school assembly? To answer such a conundrum, the individual school would have had to be the focus of the research study. On top of this, very sensitive and, probably, novel research methods might have to be employed.

When we are establishing the general and the particular, we have to define and agree on what we mean by each. Against the back cloth of a local education authority, a school is the particular. Against the general behaviours exhibited in a school, a class of students may be the particular. Within a·class, a sub-group or individual may end up being the particular. It depends what questions we ask at the outset. It depends where we draw our parameters to bracket off a part of life, establishing that the bit we have chosen is our study area or case study.

Validity and Pragmatism

As was suggested earlier, research is dominated with quasi-scientific notions of what comprises valid research. Internal validity will be tested for the kinds of research methods used, how bias was eliminated, whether the population was large enough or representative enough, whether the data analysis was sound, whether error played its part and so on.

Having been privy to many research conversations on these issues over the years, some representing formal critiques, some amounting to informal confessions, I can't recall a single event where the researcher hasn't had to excuse some aspect of the research for falling short of the design intended. It can be like angling. In those cases where the research had stuck rigorously to its bait, the big fish were simply never caught. In those cases where the big fish were caught, the researchers had pragmatically chucked away their original bait and cast around for an alternative lure. Pure research may mainly justify itself in terms of its validity, whereas applied research may mainly justify itself in terms of its utility. At the end of the day, researchers are driven by motives which assail everyone. Sufficiently successful completion of research enterprises might ensure further funding and support. Despite its rhetoric, research is riven with pragmatism and compromise. Most research activity is underfunded, underresourced and takes place against such an unstable political and social back cloth that producing any findings which might further knowledge and understanding for any audience, should be regarded as successful. Dusty shelves full of project reports which have had little or no impact on the daily lives of anyone outside the project teams concerned, abound in university offices, libraries, administrative centres and policy bureaux.

By far the best approach to dealing with validity issues is to ensure that anyone questioning the research activities undertaken can see from public reports exactly where the project team deviated from design. If the team recognise their failings and can explain how these came about, whatever findings the research produces will more likely be accepted with reasonable grace. Where research is evaluative and people's jobs are at stake, or culture is threatened, the need to come clean is even more essential. Otherwise, the findings will be ignored as the self-perceived victims of the research attack the research processes, themselves.

Validity and Naturalistic Enquiry

Given the state of things, there is no suggestion intended here, that researchers should therefore go off into the field and disregard their research design. But what they should do, is account for their decisions to leave it behind, when it fails to produce the goods. By doing so, they and we, the readers, will learn more about the pragmatics of fulfilling research briefs. We will learn more about how to deal with contingency and mess. We will also learn what might constitute validity in some of the political and social settings we have to encounter in applied research and evaluation projects.

The following is a reproduction of part of a letter from Kyriacou (1990) in the *British Education Research Association Journal*. His validity list may be helpful. Note that he is quoting Guba and Lincoln's validity tests for the kind of qualitative research being discussed in this book.

1 Prolonged engagement
2 Persistent observation
3 Triangulation (of sources, methods, investigators and theories)
4 Peer debriefing
5 Negative case analysis refining working hypothesis against more information
6 Referential adequacy (checking preliminary findings against archived 'raw')
7 Member checking (checking findings with respondents)
8 Use of thick descriptions
9 Stepwise replication (using parallel and independent analyses of half the data)
10 Carrying out an inquiry audit, focusing on all aspects of how the study was conducted
11 Using a review panel
12 Keeping a reflexive journal (daily diary about 'self' and 'method')

One can see that these criteria for reliable or justifiable research are quite different from the sorts of criteria with which research traditionally is associated. They are criteria which have been empirically derived from repeated research work. They are truer to the processes of induction in that it is through the inductive approach to establishing understanding that they have been derived.

When taken in association with the research criteria in chapter 3 concerning ethical validity, a whole new dimension is created for understanding the parameters under which observations in natural settings, operate.

Postscript

The choice is always the same. You can make your model more complex and more faithful to reality, or you can make it simpler and easier to handle. Only the most naive scientist believes that the perfect model is the one that perfectly represent reality. Such a model would have all the drawbacks of a map as large as the city it represents, a map depicting every park, every street, every building, every tree, every pothole, every inhabitant, and every map. Were such a map possible, its specificity would defeat its purpose to generalise and abstract. Mapmakers highlight such features as their clients choose. Whatever their purpose, maps and models must simplify as much as they mimic the world. (Gleick, 1987, pp. 278–9)

6　Checking It Out

By an antirepresentationalist account I mean one which does not view knowledge as a matter of getting reality right, but rather as a matter of acquiring habits of action for coping with reality. (Rorty, 1991, p. 1)

The Memory of the Video of the Methodology of the Research?

I have an early research recollection of a 1970s Open University video which compared two researchers' approaches to classroom observation. A non too exact descriptor of one would be the ethnographer whilst the other might be loosely termed the scheduler. If I remember the two protagonists accurately, John Elliott symbolized the former and Maurice Galton the latter. Visual images (now flickering like a silent movie because I can only invent what was said) presented Elliott sitting up close to groups of pupils, making field notes and asking them questions about what they thought they were doing and Galton sitting back and ticking off behaviours at a distance on an extensive chart. Whilst the content of Elliott's work was, no doubt, phenomenological, the speed of Galton's ticking was truly phenomenal. I remember showing the video to teachers and their expressions of alarm. Whilst Elliott's work seemed too cryptic and relied upon his own internal codification, Galton's seemed too complex and relied upon external codification.

What is the point of this memory? I don't think now — though I was possibly persuaded it was so then — that the two approaches were that different. What begins as an attempt to tease out subjectivity from objectivity begins to founder under a little analysis. Take the Galton position. . . .

The Galton Position?

He, no doubt, constructed his classroom schedule (I seem to remember it was called ORACLE) as a result of a lot of classroom enquiry. The items on his extensive lists were probably culled from extensive observation. At the point when he felt there was little else that **could** be looked for, he finished his preparations and began to apply the instrument. Whilst, allowing, for the moment, that the exercise could be likened to train spotting (although done at remarkable speed) and, therefore, reasonably objective, the whole process can be seen to have an interpretative base. Differentiation of pupil's behaviours, for example. Is looking out of the window an act of reflection on the subject at hand or is it an expression of digression? Is raising the hand an act of knowing or an act of appeasement or something else again? Is a pupil's kick premeditated, accidental or retaliatory and so on. Does being bent over an exercise book denote concentration, even when an exercise is being satisfactorily completed? Exactly what behaviours can be said to be unambiguous? The physical incarnation of pupils' wilful acts can be catalogued but the mental correlation for each remains a matter for interpretation

Take the following relatively straightforward example:

co-operative group work	Pupil A	Pupil B	Pupil C	Pupil ---> D
giving advice				
seeking advice				
giving opinion				
seeking opinion				
giving practical help				
receiving practical help				
working independently				
other				

Look at the bipolarity of *giving advice* and *taking advice*. Pupil A leans over to her friend, pupil B and asks,

Is this how you do it?

Pupil B looks blankly at the proffered book. Suddenly, she leans to her own exercise book and copies what is in A's book.

Is this giving or receiving? Is it both? I have friends who can never receive advice unless its presented, disguised in another form. Pupil A knows pupil B is in difficulty and is actually offering advice. Pupil A is actually in difficulty and is genuinely seeking corroboration for her approach. And so on. Wittgenstein (1953) would say that the communication can only be understood in terms of the agreed language codes, the nuance of the language game they are playing. For the scheduler like Galton, interpretations are bound to occur. As Wittgenstein shows, these acts may be arbitrary:

> 32   Someone coming into a strange country will sometimes learn the language of the inhabitants from ostensive definitions that they give him; and he will often have to guess the meaning of these definitions; and will **guess** sometimes right, sometimes wrong.

So, the items on a schedule contain their own ambiguities and are, anyway, installed on the list by a researcher's developed sense of significance (Sanger, 1985). Galton must include some items as having import and exclude others as having little. Every schedule is based upon some explicit or hidden order of classification. Such categorizations are based upon similarities and distinctions   otherwise how does the researcher mark out the behaviours s/he sees? Foucault (1989), in his preface to *The Order of Things*, describes how the usual logics of classification are undermined amusingly by Borges, the South American writer:

> This passage quotes a 'certain Chinese encyclopaedia' in which it is written that 'animals are divided into: (a) belonging to the Emperor, (b) embalmed, (c) tame, (d) sucking pigs, (e) sirens, (f) fabulous, (g) stray dogs, (h) included on the present classification, (i) frenzied, (j) innumerable, (k) drawn with a very fine camel hair brush, (l) *et cetera*, (m) having just broken the water pitcher, (n) that from a long way off look like flies'. In the wonderment of this taxonomy, the thing we apprehend in one leap, the thing that, by means of the fable, is demonstrated as the exotic charm of another system of thought, is the limitation of our own, the stark impossibility of thinking *that*. (p. XV)

All schedules are limited in what they can achieve because they are limited in their very construction by the classificatory act itself, as well as being continually undermined by the slippery nature of language. To complete these schedules in the heat of action puts extra pressure upon the researcher. It is surprising how the imperative of ticking boxes against a stop watch can inflict a brutal blow against our sense of free will! Here are boxes, choices must be made and ticks inserted. If there is doubt, do we stop and consider each box? Or do we tick because ticking is what we are here for? We are only obeying the orders of the schedule. If someone else constructed the schedule, would the 'picture' emerging from the ticks be similar to or different from the one in Galton's? If someone else was ticking in my place, would their ticking amount to the same picture? It is an axiom of checklists and, indeed, various other research instruments, that they are self-justificatory in the first instance. And self-fulfilling in the second. In other words, the logic of their construction is dependent upon the research goals that underpin their construction. It is a logic of the known rather than the unknown, of the established rather than the disestablished, of the theoretical rather than the atheoretical. The power to surprise is limited to the order or degree of difference within the known set of relations. That is, for example, *how much* pupil time is spent preparing to do an exercise rather than doing it, or *to what degree* the teacher favours boys rather than girls.

Galton might argue, and perhaps did, that his extensive presence in classrooms enabled him to differentiate behaviours. He was no longer the stranger that Wittgenstein portrayed. He had collected some of the clothes of the ethnographer en route. He had the advantage of some of Elliott's approaches as well as the relative objectivity of ORACLE. What then are the advantages of Elliott's position?

The Elliott Position?

The image is of someone sitting on the rim of the theatre of action, taking it all in, making occasional forays on to the stage in order to ask why or what or where. A knot of pupils getting on with classroom business and the adult researcher's face gravely looking on. Does he have a notebook? Or is it all internalized? I remember Malcolm Bradbury, the critic and novelist, saying to a group of us that he'd have to leap off to the toilet in order to write down his observations of a party. Let me remember him as having a notebook. I would imagine that he, too, spends enough time in the classroom to become familiar with the discourse and also familiar to the children so that they don't notice him that much. Since there has been discussion of ethnography elsewhere (chapter 1), I'll be short. Whatever goes on in Elliott's head is hidden from us. Only his notes, which I can't remember seeing, and his analysis can eventually become visible. Whatever his category system is it is invisible — even from him? Well, he may have a semi-structured approach and in his notebook there may be guidance notes on what to look for. He may write down verbatim comments to illuminate his observations. On other occasions he may have his tape recorder. But, whatever, he symbolizes a more interactive, up close, instinctive **human** observer. And the logic that underpins his work, the consequent category system and the interpretative processes he operates by, remain the mysteries of his profession. Just as we cannot check Galton's ticks, only his statistical analysis of them, so we can't check Elliott's capacity to process and interpret interactions, only his analysis of them. Both Galton's and Elliott's capacity to persuade us in the way that they write their reports on classroom life tend to be the major factor in our acceptance or rejection of their research. For persuasion read trust. And trust is based on a recognition that such things are possible and fit with our own experience. The more they don't fit, the more evidence we need to shift our mental sets. And we're back to the nature of evidence again and how it is sought and what vehicles are used to carry it out of life and through the mind of the researcher to us, the audience. So, do researchers tell us viable versions of truth or do they do as the architect does in the following:

There was a fence with spaces you
Could look through if you wanted to.

An architect who saw this thing
Stood there one summer evening

Took out the spaces with great care
And built a castle in the air.

The fence was utterly dumbfounded-
Each post stood there with nothing round it.

A sight most terrible to see-
They charged it with indecency

The architect then ran away
To Afric- or Americ-ay.
(Christian Morgenstern *The Fence* in Hughes and Brecht, 1976)

Or do researchers, as Rorty would wish, seek to help us to develop good habits all the better to cope with reality? Does this make a difference to how I judge the memory of that Open University videotape? I think so. It makes me throw away my prejudices about checklists and their overworked relation to reification, scientism or positivism.

Why can checklists be Good Things?

Before examples are given of differing approaches to capturing social life with predetermined category sheets clutched in one hand and ballpoint pens in the other, an elaborate answer to the above question.

Having worked with groups of would-be researchers over many years, I tend to agree with Rorty's line about not worrying too much over the discrepancies between research reconstructions and the realities that helped precipitate them. Rather, the issue lies with the power of these reconstructions to act as catalysts for seeing anew, taking action, or changing individuals' patterns of engagement with that reality.

So, whatever the research artefact, its significance lies within its power to enrich debate, challenge our suppositions, or try new forms of action, not necessarily in its lepidopteristic capacity to pin reality to a board. Thus it is that details of working practices, whether they are in the form of tick sheets or narrative accounts, tend to be pored over animatedly by the workers, themselves.

As researchers, we will always have to defend our methods and show that we have tried to iron out the worst excesses of bias, error and ambiguity. We always will have to show that we can articulate the methodological problems we face. It is often easier for critics of research to attack methods of data collection and the representativeness of the sample chosen than respond to the findings.

Observation Counts

One of the most basic ways of collecting data is by counting how many times something occurs. We are surprisingly astonished by this process. It's often that we are unaware of it. We become aware of the more obtrusive forms of repetition in peoples' behaviour such as stammers, swearing, tics, or dress sense. But counts of less obvious elements of behaviour throw up interesting data that challenge us, often at very deep levels:

- time spent at each bed in a hospital ward;
- number of times the nurse touches coma patients;
- lengths of queues at teachers' desks;
- elapsed silences after teacher asks questions, before (usually) teacher interrupts;
- girls asked questions in class as opposed to boys;
- teacher talk as opposed to student talk;
- transition time between lessons;
- boys as opposed to girls punished with detention;
- gender differences at a range of arcade machines.

These may be counted using five-barred gates, prearranged sheets, stopwatches or whatever. Provided the results are presented clearly (often together with the rough copy used to count in the first place to show that they have not been glossed), simple counts can have very desirable effects. For example, how does a teacher react to the following data from her classroom?

> Analysis of transcript of class discussion
>
> Teacher talk = 75% of word count
> Pupil talk = 25% of word count

Or this data from a hospital ward?

> Average time spent with coma patients = 12 mins
> Average time spent with conscious patients = 23 mins

The major impact is usually for participants to ask the question, *why? Why is this so?* And, secondly, *what are the consequences?* Usually, this leads to attempts at more complex research of a hypothesis-testing type. In other words, participants want to collect evidence about their teaching in a more focussed way, altering their behaviour and initiating new strategies to understand and remediate the import of the original checklist's analysis.

So, checklists or tick sheets do act as catalysts. Providing they are straightforward and relatively unambiguous, they can give an indication of the basic structure of events. What they do not do, of course, is indicate the *quality* of those events. We have no notion of the intrinsic interest of the class in the teacher's talk in the first example, or whether the teacher is deliberately providing fuel for later debate. Or whether pupils are asking questions which are relatively profound and requiring the teacher to give elaborated replies. We don't know the tactility of contact nurses have with patients in the second example. They may hold the hands of coma patients but not the conscious ones. The amount of time spent with the coma patients may be double that normally spent with such individuals in other wards. The important thing about checklists is to ensure that they are constructed to gather the particular data the researcher requires. Take the following:

> Teacher's questioning in 30 minute period:
> Open   2
> Closed   12

If the teacher was persuaded that such a totting up represents an indictment of her teaching style, a little thought might make her think again. A qualitative analysis of the questions that teachers' ask may show that closed questions sometimes lead to open debate — and that open questions shut off debate. For example, look at this piece of transcript from an FE lecturer's classroom: The number of so-called closed questions and interventions are legion. However, prior to this extract, the videotape from which this is culled, shows ten minutes of non-interactive group work, with students reading from prepared texts to a group which appears apathetic to the whole process. The lecturer's interjections here (overriding the appointment of a student chairperson), seem to change the whole ethos of the event.

Lecturer: (to Chairman) May I ask a question . . . may I . . . can I just go over it again and answer this one? (to Ronnie) You said that **power-sharing was shared by everyone** except the IRA —
Ronnie: — was accepted . . . the general idea.
Lecturer: Now is that right . . . what you said?
Ronnie: According to the video I watched, yes. Don't you think so?

Lecturer: Well, would you say it again and just look round the room and see if people agree with you.

(Hoots from the rest of the group. General playing up to the camera.)

Lecturer: 'Cause I'm flabbergasted by that. What did you say about power sharing?
Ronnie: I said that power sharing failed in 1974.
Lecturer: That's correct.
Ronnie: (Quoting) 'This option is accepted by all parties except the IRA.'
Lecturer: *Hrrmmm!* I think somebody ought to say something about that. . . . UPROAR.
I think somebody ought to say something about that. . . .
Fred: *Are you sure you got that right?*
(RUMPUS)

(Lecturer brings in Fred)

Fred: I was just thinking are you sure you got that right. I don't remember hearing anything about that . . . maybe it was suggested . . .
Ronnie: It's just something I wrote down, off the video . . .
Lecturer: (cues in Mr Ormsby.)
Lecturer: Right I think we ought to hear Mr Ormsby (Sam).
Ronnie: If you remember there was a pie chart with various sections of a jigsaw puzzle and they featured each of them in for each of the **five** options.
Sam: That wasn't the point. The point of that is that the IRA wouldn't have discussions with them, not that they wouldn't agree to that. It's that they wouldn't discuss with them because they use violence.
Ronnie: Oh, I don't know nothing about it.
Lecturer: Yes, Sam, could you? I don't think Ronnie was wrong, but it's a matter of emphasis, of interpretation . . . would you just . . .
Sam: — the power sharing thing . . . I don't think the Ulster Unionists would agree with that for a start . . .
Lecturer: I'm sure that's right, that's correct. The big stumbling block to power sharing is not the IRA, the Ulster Unionists. I think that's correct Philip but could you just put Ronnie right and say what did Ronnie misinterpret?
Sam: I think he misinterpreted literally the pie chart.
Lecturer: That's right.
Sam: The IRA were left out of it, but that was not because they didn't want to be in it. It's because they (Unionists) didn't . . . wouldn't discuss with them because they (IRA) didn't have

a political force at that time. They do have now — Sinn
Fein. They (Unionists) still won't talk to them either.
(Sanger, 1989a)

Thus, we can see that open and closed questions and statements can only be
judged to be so *in their consequences.* The earlier checklist showing the number
of open and closed questions may not have gathered what was intended.

A central tension in checklist instruments, then, will always be between
subjectivity and objectivity, which in turn lead to different kinds of judgment.
Having agreed that there will always be an element of ambiguity, even in the
most rigorous of instruments, the observer should make do and allow for
some margin of error. In the following example, that margin increases:

Tick the space which describes your line manager's behaviour

Friendly						Unfriendly
Considerate						Thoughtless
Encouraging						Discouraging
Interested in your views						Interested in own ideas

Graphic rating scales have a highly subjective element to them. However, they
supply data, which, triangulated over a number of individuals, gives an indication of ability, competency or personal quality.

In the end, it is probably best to think of checklists as cool and dispassionate ways of collecting information. Providing the language is unambiguous, the task is straightforward and is not composed of too many choices, then
useful data can be gathered. Variations can be developed for different purposes. A teacher I worked with in Nottinghamshire produced the following:

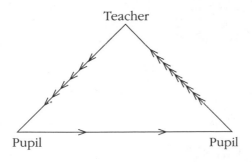

in order to be able to move round her classroom and note when pupils questioned each other and when individual pupils questioned her. Of course, this simple device worked well for her because she knew the kinds of questions that she was interested in. She could discount those that she felt were insignificant such as requests for resources or social chat and concentrate upon requests for task-related information. As you see from the diagram, most requests are directed at her, so that, if her desire is to have more autonomy in the classroom, she will need to employ some innovative strategies to ease dependency on the teacher.

Of Sociograms

This triangle is a simple and more stylized version of a sociogram. Sociograms are mapping tools for interaction. You have to create a map which represents where people are sitting or standing. The problems with sociograms is that they are designed to deal in slightly greater complexity with human interaction — but can only be used with stationary targets. You win some and you lose some. It becomes increasingly difficult to handle a sociogram as the number of people being observed increases, too. Below is a sociogram which relates to a staff nurse's concern that she was not managing to inform her nurse team, fully, concerning their rota duties. It roughly represents the seating arrangement. The staff nurse is at the mouth of the horse-shoe, the nurses are lettered alphabetically. The observer sits in one corner, bottom right.

Verbal communication between staff nurse and nursing teams about to go on duty

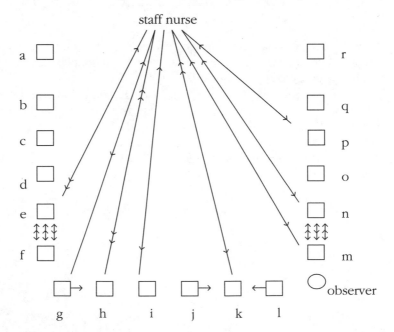

What would she gain from the diagram? The arrows show the direction of communication from speaker to receiver. The number of arrowheads depict the number of communications. Again, the quality of the communication is not the issue. However, in this case, the sociogram confirmed her concerns about nurses m, n, e and f, who frequently 'got things wrong' and had to come back to her for further information. Also, she became aware of how her briefings were fielded by the group: who tended to be active and who passive. It led her to reorganize the proceedings.

The relationship of the sociogram with the checklist is obvious. Greater information can be added to the map, by, for instance, inserting times of questions next to arrowheads. This can show whether there is a pattern of interaction over a session. In schools there would be an expectation that questions would flow around task-setting activity or the introduction of a complex new concept and then ease off as students become immersed in their work. From then on, questions might be more sporadic. Again, there might be another burst at the end of the session, when homework is set.

A sequence of sociograms can begin to show the relationships which exist within groups. Gregarious individuals have arrows pointing at and away from them. The withdrawn remain arrowless. The distracters have arrowheads pointing towards others. All of which can be useful when trying to optimize learning, since where people sit can have a dramatic consequence for their learning. These sort of data can be even more useful to professionals such as social workers or analysts, when the groups concerned have been brought together for therapeutic purposes.

Whilst sociograms are communication maps, they don't denote the environment against which such activity takes place. People are foregrounded and there is no sense of background. Cinema technique today (also enjoyed by the camcorder user) enables the amateur or professional director to shift focus from the foreground figure to something or someone in the background, which, until this point, has remained part of the blur. When sociograms switch in this way, interesting possibilities emerge.

Stages of observation

If the researcher knows the backdrop to events, s/he can watch how participants, like characters in a play, interact with the environment. To do this you must make a map of the environment, as if you were a theatre director. Then, when the actors emerge, you can plot their paths around the stage and develop a sense of their choreography. Take the map of the classroom below:

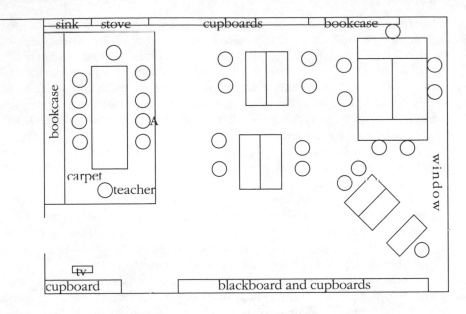

By creating this map, the observer can plot various activities within the stage set. Take pupil A, for example. He can be followed round the classroom, a form of pupil pursuit and his use of resources, including other pupils and the teacher, noted. A completed, half-hour observation of pupil A, might look like this:

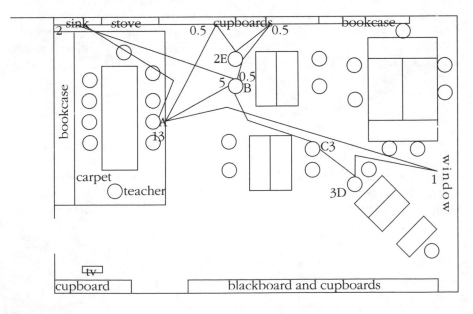

Pupil A has visited pupils B, C, D and E. The numbers by each letter or stopping-off point represent how long he remained there. Note that he stays at the resources (water, paints) for a total of three minutes. He is at his desk for thirteen minutes and with other pupils for the rest, roughly half his time in the painting session. The researcher might use a few such maps at the same time, following a small number of students round the classroom. If there is only one student being followed, then it is easier and more productive merely to write a narrative, detailed pupil pursuit. Using several sheets can build up an interesting sample of classroom activity. Issues such as distraction/disruption can be investigated, as well as transition from one activity to another, social engagement, general classroom management such as whether resources are positioned to facilitate easy access without queuing, gender interaction and so on. Maps also act as a useful mnemonic in a researcher's fieldnotes.

Postscript

I recall a story told me when I was a choir boy — just before I was relieved of my surplice for unruly conduct. Canon Tillard said that certain scientists were setting themselves up as equal to God. They had a wager with the chief priest of a certain land that whatever God could do, they could also do.

The priest took a seed of cress and said, 'Can you make that?'

They smiled and took the seed away. After careful analysis they had produced a check list of the seed's molecular structure. By itemising the ingredients they were able to build an indentical seed. They presented this to the priest. 'See, we have done what we said we would do. Now, can you tell any difference between our seed and God's?'

It was the priest who smiled now. He placed their seed and another on damp sponges. A little later he announced, 'This is God's seed. That is yours.' A small root had emerged from one of the seeds.

7   Seeing Through The Interview

'Does the literal truth matter?'
She thought about that. 'To the person to whom it happened.'
(A Compass Error, Sybille Bedford)

I wrote a paper with Barry MacDonald in the early eighties about interviewing. In qualitative research it represents the third leg of the *observation-interview-documentation* triptych and probably is the most significant of the three, judging by the sheer volume of data generated by this method and the degree to which it is preferred in determining eventual research and evaluation judgments. What we tried to do was to contrast the approaches and consequences of using a tape recorder or fieldnotes for interview recording purposes. At that stage, we could not find much deep analysis of the technologizing of the interview process.

> One is tempted to conclude that the interview process is indescribable or unjustifiable, apparently self-taught, probably idiosyncratic, perhaps not worth talking about. Even if one pieces together the relevant fragments from the voluminous output of a methodologist like Lou Smith, who more than anyone else has described his fieldwork behaviour in terms of its underlying intellectual purposes, structures, and processes (see particularly Smith, 1981), the impression remains that a rather important instrument of evaluative enquiry is characterised by an unusual degree of normative latitude. (MacDonald and Sanger, 1982, p. 175)

Interviews take place within an observational context. This chapter focuses upon the interplay of the two and freely uses the format and some of the writing of the original paper as a starting point. However, the decade which has intervened makes its present use a tool for dialogue between two quite distinct research positions. The one I held back then and the current, rather less formalized anarchy.

As was pointed out in that paper, debate takes place constantly between researchers concerning their research practices, though these are rarely transformed into methodological papers. Nevertheless, different profiles of interviewing practice begin to emerge and take shape, the blooms of a hitherto secret garden. And what becomes immediately evident is that this secret garden is no collective farm. Even in research centres with a shared rhetoric of intent and consensual canons of criticisms, the varying prosecutions of intent and interpretations of the canons reveal a disturbingly wide range of modi operandi. Of course, we all agree that interviewing should be consistent with the naturalistic imperative-to generate public knowledge of forms of professional activity which derives from, consists of, or is coextensive with private knowledge. And of course, we all agree that interviews, the best method we have for getting access to this private knowledge, should be effective, fair, and valid. Such agreements do go some way toward defining the boundaries of the permissible, but they fall short of resolving our epistemological, political and technical differences. These differences shape our procedures, our roles, and ultimately our products, in ways that are not widely understood. This chapter tries to provide a window to what tends to be a private debate, emphasizing the place of the observer within interview activity. In the course of writing it, one reason for the paucity of methodological debate became quite clear. The issues are complex and interpenetrating, and the range of practice is so wide as to defy unchangeable categorization for purposes of comparison and contrast.

In the first place I will, as Barry MacDonald and I did then, concentrate more upon unstructured and semi-structured interviews. Structured interviews may be regarded as oral questionnaires and as such, have much in common with checklists in chapter 6. In the second place, the discussion is organised around whether the interviewer should take notes or tape record the interview. Both are observational instruments of a kind in that they record the world. Whilst tape recording would appear to release the observer more than note taking, the actuality is more complex. At the centre of the debate are the different demands of evaluation and research, too. The former demands pragmatism and expediency in order to push through an agenda which has consequences for people's professional lives. The latter, whilst ideally less pressured and less likely to be hamstrung by the original aims of a project or programme, has a context which still must embrace an ethical responsibility. Where there are differences, these will be teased out.

For qualitative research, as has already been stressed, the interview, even more than observation, is the predominant means of data gathering. Its flexibility and negotiability make it uniquely attractive to evaluators who usually need to gather many different kinds of data in a short span of time, or researchers who are pursuing longer term goals involving human action in organizational or other life. But even in quantificatory research studies, test batteries are predicated on interviews designed to yield contingency data. In other words, the interview is now a commonplace instrument of program evaluation and other studies.

A great deal of this interviewing is known as 'unstructured'. The term has no consensual meaning. At the one end of the spectrum of users are those who, armed with a range of programme interests, problems, issues, perhaps even conclusions, mean by it only that they do not know what line of questioning they will pursue until they have a chance to see what kind of information is available. 'Unstructured' in this sense means no more than tactical opportunism. At the other end, where most qualitative researchers are located, 'unstructured' connotes an epistemological sensitivity to the terms in which interviewees understand their experience, and an intent, in some sense, to keep faith with their biographies and agendas. Again, what is meant by keeping faith is not always clear. There is a big difference between those for whom validity inheres in the subjective, individualized organization of affect and cognition, those whose claims rest upon the strength of a literal interpretation of the term 'interview', those metatheorists who seek reconstructions of experience that account for the self-knowledge of others and, finally, those for whom the interview is an artefact, symbolizing political and powerful forces within culture or history. Most would agree that validity depends upon inter subjective agreement but would differ about the parts played by interviewees, interviewer, and audiences in securing and validating the data of social life. Some invoke scientific labels to indicate where they stand on this rather daunting issue, but it is not all clear how evaluative interviewers of, say, phenomenological persuasion would differ from, say, symbolic interactionists, post-structuralists, ethnomethodologists, existentialists, linguistic ethnoscientists, or ethnographers of communication. But as evaluators of social programmes or researchers of organizational life, concerned with the acquisition and transfer of knowledge of human action, we all have at least a sense of the problematics of enquiry that shapes and sensitizes our practice.

For the evaluative researcher, the intrinsic problems of interview data are compounded by the sociopolitical circumstances in which he/she tries to resolve them. The project or programme evaluator operates in a context of persuasion, a contest for resources in which his/her role is to provide knowledge for allocation decisions. With truth and consequence so intertwined, disinterest, which might help, is a scarce commodity. And that's not all. The interviewer has to be fair to those whose interests are at risk, and this commitment can seriously restrict the pursuit of private knowledge.

When an evaluator, for example, constructs an interview sample, that sample has to represent the constituency of interests generated by the programme if he/she is to avoid the charge of taking sides. Programme constituencies tend to be large and varied and so must be the sample. Such evaluators rarely have the time, resources, or freedom to develop the kind of intimate, friendly relationship with respondents that is commonly advocated by social scientists as a precondition of productive and valid interaction. Prominent programme actors apart, the evaluative interview tends to be a one-off, hit-or-miss, encounter between relative strangers. Can it do more than offer the stakeholders a chance to be heard? Can it do even that?

For researchers, not unduly hampered by the pragmatics of programme evaluation, there are still constraints of time and other resources, which lead the individual into a fast tailoring of the research process to suit the demands of external funding, research supervisor or in-house brief.

At some point a programme evaluator needs to know what it is like to take part in the programme and the researcher, what it is like to be part of the organization or other social activity, what meanings and significance they hold for participants, why they respond in the ways they do. The researcher or evaluator is an outsider looking in, trying to find out what it is like to be an insider. Not merely for his/her own satisfaction; he/she has to tell others. These others may be non participants, the evaluator's or researcher's various 'publics'. Or they may be the participants themselves, users and receivers as well as givers of this knowledge. The evaluator and researcher has, therefore, both outsider and insider audiences in mind. He/she usually already knows a lot about the surface features of the research population. The evaluator knows a lot too about patterns of interaction between programme participants, which participants have had opportunities to observe and judge other participants, who is likely to know what about the programme. But the evaluator knows too that these surface features are more constitutive of public performance than of private experience, and are heavily shaped by programme scripts, professional norms, personal image management, and structures of account-ability. The evaluator wants, assuming that his/her audiences need, a better understanding than these indices give of why the program in action is the way it is. In these circumstances, the evaluator looks to the unstructured interview to reveal the dark side of the programme moon. Meanwhile, the researcher seeks a comparable depth of understanding of the motivations, influences and social contexts of participants in action.

Unstructured interviewing is peculiarly appropriate for such purposes, arguably being indispensable for those who seek to represent the concerns and interests of those they research and evaluate. In principle it allows all parties to participate in the generation of an agenda and permits the inter-viewee to be proactive in that process. The extensive and effective use of such interviews could help to redress the imbalance of interests that invariably ensues from the circumstances and sources of interviewers agendas. But un-structured interviewing promises more; it appears to offer a means of getting to the nub of the 'information for understanding' problem. With rare excep-tions, and to a greater or lesser extent, participants fail in many of their aspi-rations. They stumble, they seize up, they get subverted, emasculated, rejected, diverted, diluted, or otherwise run out of steam. Even those programme evalu-ators who preconceive their major task as the demonstration of goal accom-plishment, end up casting around for unanticipated benefits and trying to explain shortfalls in targeted outcomes. The development of more sensitive and durable models of intervention has much to gain from efforts to map and understand what happens to people in professional life, and the unstructured interview is the means by which underestimated or unanticipated dimensions of program experience may be probed.

To look in detail at interviewing and the place of observation in it, this presentation will explore one seemingly insignificant variable, the choice be-tween tape recording and note taking as the means of recording. We originally said 'seemingly insignificant' not because it seemed so to us, but because the few published guides of that time that made reference to it paid scant attention to it. To quote Guba and Lincoln (1981)

> For most of this kind of interviewing we recommend notepads and written notes; tape recorders can make one a victim of the 'laters'- Iater I will listen to these tapes,

One might add, 'Later I will analyze these data.' Here, typically, tape recording and note taking are treated as if they were alternative means of generating an identical product rather than generators of different kinds of encounters with divergent products.

Johnson (1975), reviewing his field study of social welfare officers, notes briefly two phenomena that are central to our analysis of interviewing options. At one point in his research he had the opportunity to compare written fieldnotes with cassette recordings of the observed events. He writes:

> First, the master field notes reflected an attempt to recapture all the statements of a particular worker as he presented the facts of a case and the diagnosis reached. Grammatical and syntactical structures, as I recalled them, had also been recorded. The transcripts, however, illustrated my illusions. They revealed only my grammar and syntax.

If this degree of discrepancy is characteristic of a committed and sensitive observer, what can we reasonably expect of the notes of the more involved interviewer? Does it matter? One distinguished sociologist, questioned on this issue at a gathering of naturalistic enquirers, shrugged off the problem as a pedantic quibble, with words to the effect, 'I don't care if he actually said what I say he said. The point is he might have said it.' (I leave to the reader the enigma of the status of a recalled exchange that was neither taped nor written down.) Some of those present were shocked by the response, others nodded knowingly. Whose truth is it, anyway? Later in the same review Johnson returns to the comparison, this time to attack the taped record.

> When I listened to the cassette recordings of home visits, on several occasions I realized that I knew certain things about the actions that had not been stated in so many words. This is not to imply I had to read between the lines of the transcripts or review them in an ironic or metaphorical manner to understand them. It is to say some of the crucial features of the action were not expressed verbally.

Such observations and reactions introduce one set of issues and possibilities that need to be taken into account when we choose how and what to record when we interview. Fidelity, accuracy, validity, even authenticity are at risk. But there is another set of issues and possibilities, linked to the first set but not addressed by the comments cited. A decision to take notes or to tape record significantly influences the nature of the social process of interviewing, in particular the generative power of the encounter. In what follows, both the necessary and the arguable differences between a conversation in which the interviewer writes things down and a conversation which is automatically recorded, leaving the interviewer apparently free to do other things, is pursued.

For the interviewer, the unstructured interview poses three serious problems. The first is how to achieve a penetrative conversation with relative strangers, often in a short space of time. The second problem, given a solution to the first, is how to be fair to the interviewee whose interests are at stake. Striking a balance between the 'right to know' and the individual's right to some measure of protection is a central issue in the politics and ethics of research. In unstructured interviewing the individual faces the maximum risk of personal exposure, and this means that the two problems referred to are at least uncomfortably juxtaposed and arguably indissoluble. The third problem, given a 'solution' to the first two, is 'what claims to truth are associable with the results?' The case for any system of conducting, recording, interpreting and reporting such interviews must therefore address these problems and offer a resolution.

Although the choice between tape and notes can be seen as a discrete issue of ad hoc preference, the choice is better understood as an issue embedded in differing rationales, and to begin the dissection of the two interviewing practices it is necessary to outline the reasoning that we invoked, in that earlier paper, in their defence. The case for tape recording is made within a particular view of the interviewer's role in a liberal-democratic society. The case for note taking takes account of this view, is sympathetic to its concerns and values, but offers an alternative response to the problems of research fieldwork. The two positions are comprehensive in that they address the purposes, values, and aspirations of research and evaluation enquiry and try to show how procedures and methods are related to these. At the same time, the overall advocacy is tempered by consciousness of deficiency. The attempt here is to have more attention paid to the underlying issues, not converts to a particular practice.

The Case for Tape Recording

The unstructured interview is the means by which, throughout a constituency of stakeholders in a particular programme or professional or other organizational activity, the interviewer promotes the manufacture of a trading commodity (private data, personal experience, individual evaluations) that will constitute the basis of his/her subsequent efforts to achieve exchange (reporting). Within this perspective the autonomy of the interviewee is respected, and the principle of reciprocity guides the interviewer in trade-offs between constituents. The separation of the data generation and data reporting phases of the process is essential to the operation, as is the construction of an interview sample that represents the interviewer's agenda of 'interests'. In its strongest form this conception of interviewing derives from a political philosophy that stresses the individual as decision maker and the dangers of both bureaucratic and academic control of social enquiry.

Choosing priorities of focus, of issues, of audience-is clearly a headache for such interviewers. After all, everybody has an 'interest' in the research or evaluation. Some have more to gain and lose. Potency of, and accountability for, action are prime factors in the interviewer's response to the problem of how to conduct the interview. So is demand, positive and negative. So is access. Evaluators and researchers can only look at what they are allowed to see, and visas can be hard to get. They have to honour their contracts too, and these may preempt both initial and emergent options. The independence we like to associate with both research and evaluation is difficult to secure and maintain in this context of multiple constraints.

Nevertheless, all interviewers carry into their work a view of their service that determines how they exploit the available or negotiable areas of discretion. The particular conception of this service that was outlined in the earlier paper was one to which one of the writers (MacDonald, 1976) had attached the label 'democratic', a deliberately provocative title intended to focus attention on the political function of evaluation. Democratizing research and evaluation (making the service more consonant with the principles of the liberal democratic state) commits the interviewer to a particular political view of what he/she is about. It makes central and problematic the means by which, and the degree to which, private knowledge should become public knowledge. It means respect for persons as both givers and receivers of information. It means enhancing the possibility of the widest possible debate about matters of common interest and consequence. In this sense an evaluation report can be seen as fulfilling the function of foreshadowing (rather than preempting or concluding) a debate about what should happen next. A research report can be seen to be illuminating context and issues rather than seeking 'findings'. That is the justification for the apparently inconclusive nature of such reports. I am taking the backdrop to research and evaluation in this chapter, still to be that of the liberal democracy, for want of something better. The aspirations to do research and evaluation which informs without injury is a powerful guiding impulse. Nevertheless, there are dangers in the very notions of liberal democracy. Foucault's (1989) work on how truth and justice are coercive concepts of the status quo, need keeping in view.

Given these aspirations and focusing now on the unstructured interview, we can say that words are important, what the interviewee says. Non-verbal communications are interpretations of the observer. Creating the conditions in which the interviewee says what he/she means, means what he/she says, says what he/she thinks, and thinks about what he/she says, are the major tasks of the interviewer. Self-representation in transportable form is the aim. The place of observation is to cross-reference words with the capturing of consonant or dissonant images.

The case for the tape recorder is embedded in these concerns and values.

At one level it rests upon a conception of the interview as a creative process that demands of the interviewer, full commitment to the generation of data. The use of the recorder allows postponement of those roles (processing and reporting) that would seriously limit this commitment or otherwise inhibit the interchange. In their place, notes may be made concerning non-verbal responses to the significance of the word exchange. A procedural corollary of this aspiration, dealt with elsewhere (chapter 4) is that the data so generated belongs in the first instance to the interviewee. Its subsequent use by the interviewer for the purpose of informing others has to be negotiated with the interviewee-owner. The presence of the recorder means that the interviewer is free to concentrate on one task-production. Relieved of any immediate need to edit the communication, to select, marshal, and codify what he/she hears and sees, the interviewer can listen to all that is said, observe all the non-verbal communications, and develop a person-to-person dynamic without the hindrance of constant reminders of ultimate purpose and role. The tape recorder in this sense seems to offer the best opportunity of realizing the intentions of the unstructured interview. That is to evoke and develop the interviewee's affective and cognitive experience of the topic of interest. Precisely because the encounter is not experienced by the interviewee as instrumental to the purposes of others, precisely because he/she is not compelled to produce the immediately negotiable public account, the interview offers a rare opportunity to explore, with an unusually attentive and interested listener, his/her own realms of meaning and significance. It is these realms of meaning — the private experience and evaluation of public life-that the interviewer needs to represent in subsequent dialogues on policy and practice.

The record is essential for subsequent phases of a researcher's work. It guarantees the availability of an accurate chronicle of the verbal component of the interview, a total record of what both participants said, together with the possible interleaving of how the individual reacted and acted. Although it is unlikely to be reproduced in full in an report, the record is the basis of subsequent representations of the interview and negotiations about its use. For the interviewee and for other parties who may wish to challenge or corroborate the use in context or the interpretative selection of the data, it constitutes an independent and undeniable resource. Depending upon the agreed rules governing control of the interview data, the tape may be seen as a first draft, a basis for further development as well as negotiation. Given unqualified interviewee control over the use of the interview the evaluator does, of course, risk the loss of revealing data, but interviewees may exercise this power by demonstrating a correspondingly greater sense of responsibility for securing the validity and adequacy of the data. Experience shows that programme participants who have had this opportunity to ensure that their experience, concerns, and perspectives are adequately represented in final reporting (i.e., that they have had a say, not just a hearing) are much more receptive to critique of their actions and less hostile to the reporting of alternative perspectives. In short, the use of the tape recorder in the generation of a data base enables the tasks of the interviewer to be shared more effectively with many of those who are most vulnerable to the consequences. Since we have argued that the taped interview frees the interviewer to develop a more penetrative discourse and a triangulative rigour with observation, the provision of these checks and balances constitutes a necessary safeguard against misuse of the product.

Weakness of Tape Recording

It is only a partial record of the interaction and the communication — the sound component — and even this partial record will be reduced if, as usually happens, subsequent use of the record is based on transcript-words only. These verbatim accounts reveal the extent to which communication depends upon the synthesis of sound, gesture, expression, and posture. In extreme cases the word residue of the communication is unintelligible. In every case it underrepresents the communication and requires for comprehensiveness, the addition of observational notes on non-verbal features. The experienced interviewer can to some extent aid this process by prompting verbalization ('That's an interesting shrug, what does it mean exactly?'). Note-taking interviewers have a similar problem but rely on their own reading of the communication to round out incomplete sentences and non-verbalized intimations of states of mind. Facility with language, experience of self-representation, and a preference for the kind of discourse that best survives the recording filter are important variables in any research agenda, and there is a danger that tape-based representations will be skewed in favour of the most articulate. This skew can be compounded by uneven take-up on the part of interviewees of opportunities to improve the accounts they have given and to monitor their use. In many social programmes, these characteristics of interviewees will correlate with the interviewee's location in a hierarchical system and can lead to a serious distortion in reports in favour of superordinate perspectives.

Of course, ethics in research should impel the interviewer to do his/her best to counter these threats to the validity and fairness of the reports. This can be done by making sure that his/her principles and procedures are understood by all interviewees, that all have reasonable opportunities to exercise the rights accorded to them, and that those who have most difficulty in fulfilling their tasks are given most assistance. These obligations upon the interviewer lead us into consideration of a major weakness of the approach — the demands it makes of the evaluator's or researcher's time and resources. Tape based research involves a slow process and one that is costly in terms of secretarial support. It invokes a complex system of separate stages in the execution of the research or evaluation task and the maintenance over a period of time of a participant network. It is ill-suited as a major instrument of enquiry in circumstances of urgency, where information about one part of a constituency is needed quickly by another. It is messy, complicated, and exasperatingly subject to delays, even where the interviewer has negotiated agreed deadlines with interviewees. For these reasons alone it is unpopular with those who commission enquiries, and can often only be successfully advocated in circumstances where the inadequacy of managerial assumptions and forecasts is either evident or anticipated, where there is enough time to learn, or where programmes and other activities are so politically sensitive that an independent democratic approach is a necessary concession to hostile stakeholders.

The Case for Note Taking

Historically, and in disparate disciplines and paradigms, note-taken accounts of interviews have been preferred to other forms of recording in that they aspire to serve two basic functions for which other techniques are inadequate. These functions are unobtrusiveness and economy of effort. Any reference to the technology of recording by authors of case-study manuals or naturalistic inquiry methods usually prefaces a choice for note taking with some such declaration. However, note taking has a broader basis for use than just these two criteria.

The note-taking interview should be seen as a joint act of making. The interviewer is a representative of near and distant audiences and enables the interviewee to develop a case for those audiences. The fact that the data is generated in note form maintains least transformation in the process of creating the final vehicle of communication in which the data will reside. At all stages there are words on paper. These include both summaries of what has been said and what has not been spoken aloud. These, taken together in a holistic representation of the interview event. By encouraging the respondent to be privy at the outset to these stages of production, the interviewer's operations are given high and contestable profile and his/her authority, conversely, is diminished as the respondent discovers an equal control of opportunity. If, as would be ideally the case, the interviewer is able to complete his/her notes and present them the same day for comment to the respondent, then the meaning-making *process* will become much more meaningful to the respondent. And the respondent gains shared control over his/her products.

What is this mysterious process? It comprises the usually hidden, reflexive acts of interpretation, analysis, and synthesis that convert data into field notes, draft and final reports. These acts are evidenced in the written words, themselves, the syntax, the metaphors, the juxtaposition of information, the special highlighting of data, and the very act of overall summarizing. The events of the interview, visual and aural, are committed to the mnemonics of note taking. The act of note-taking is already the groundwork of theory building. Essentially, they are interwoven in a story that communicates the 'essence' of the constituency's experience. It is usually as a storyteller that the note maker achieves greatest impact.

Note taking should aspire to make the interviewee aware that he/she is not merely a source of so much recondite information but that he/she informs and educates the researcher or evaluator. The personal constructs of the interviewee are to be afforded the important significance owing to him/her by the deference exemplified in the conduct of the interview.

The interviewee becomes the subject of thoughtful effort on the part of the interviewer to be placed carefully in the unravelling scheme of social action. Note taking, at best, draws interviewer and interviewee closer in the mutuality of the event. Their developed intimacy imbues both words and syntax with information (the substantive in the interviewee's account) and with the character of the interviewee. Properly recorded notes thus become acutely analogous to the interview in its social and psychological context. For the note taker, the notes are a meaningful coding of the interview event. Providing the interviewer manages to engage the respondent in joint action, there is then every possibility that the interview can proceed to the penetrative levels that the interviewer requires. The notebook acts as a symbol of the interest and concern of the interviewer and the importance he/she ascribes to the interaction.

There is an overall pragmatic reason for choosing notes to other forms of recording during research: economy. On-site data processing and the collection of summarized information enable the researcher to keep in constant touch with the pulse of his/her operations. Analysis and synthesis leading to theory are kept within the event and are not imposed at a temporal distance, in the manner of a jigsaw, with the construction of discrete pieces of cold data. Notions of swift feedback have influenced a great deal of the work I have done in appraisal, evaluation and research. The name I coined for it was 'hot storage'. Just as witnesses have their clearest memories of events such as accidents or muggings, immediately afterwards, so interviewees or those that are being observed, require immediate feedback, for the data to resonate with the experience.

In the best of circumstances this helps to keep the researcher focused upon the here and now, the properties of the field of study, enabling later interpretations which are in tune with the idiosyncratic context rather than imposing interpretations of the data as a result of theories held, ideologies or political persuasions. Patterns of explanation that make up eventual reports, case studies, or portrayals must take account of these disparately processed, obstinately extant interview events, rather than the researcher seeking post-event coherence for a mountain of raw data and treating it piecemeal.

And what of the practical criteria that facilitate the successful interview? When to write and what to write provide the interviewer with his/her greatest challenge. Given that eye contact and general non-verbal encouragement provide the basis of sympathetic listening, recourse to notes should be minimized to a short hand. Notes are generally effective in/for the following circumstances:

- When previously undiscovered data of importance arise from the testimony of the witness.

- Data that would be difficult or impossible to triangulate in the testimonies of other witnesses.
- Metonymic statements, though obviously seriously intended, seem at variance with the expected or consistent viewpoints of individual or group.
- Statements that politically, theoretically, or situationally seem to define significant insights or attitudes of an individual or group.
- Key words whose currency gives insight to individual or group thinking.
- Key words that, for the interviewer, allow reconstruction of the depth and breadth of the interview.
- Significant facts.

The purpose of these notational forms is to make the respondent conscious of the interviewer in a service role, at ease and in control of the technology of recording. The service role becomes experientially amplified for the interviewee in the course of the event. The role is one that facilitates the respondent in developing an articulate and just explanation of his/her thinking concerning all areas of public interest.

Note taking and note making will always be a matter of highly developed skill. Every act of recording involves meaningful transformations of data. Words have a contextual clothing. Verbatim accounts do not necessarily provide accurate representation of what occurs in interviews. However, through the broad strokes of the note-taken account, much nuance, implicit and explicit, is retained, rather as in impressionism in painting; stand too close and the meaning's gone. In this way, note recordings are ideally suited to protecting the respondent against the kind of retaining mud that context-bound statements often produce. Note taking attends to the fluid process of people-in-charge. It does not hold them to particular states or attitudes or final statements but reflects the daily choices and changes that people have to make in their daily lives.

Weaknesses in Note Taking

Note taking has some very obvious problems associated with it. In many ways these problems combine to demonstrate that, at the stage of recording data, factors such as accuracy, fairness, and appropriateness may be largely decided by the interviewer's skill with the technology.

The most obvious practical difficulty that note taking presents to the smooth generation of data is in its capacity to be distracting to the respondent. Handled badly: breaks of eye contact to rush to the note pad, a slow scrawl holding back a respondent's flow or even the pained look of the interviewer realizing that he/she is suffering data overload; and the interview devolves into non-penetrative irritation. If the respondent does not dry up, then he/she may become 'coopted' to the needs of the interviewer by picking up cues from pen movement, speaking selectively and pausing dramatically to allow assimilation and recording. Lack of penetration becomes heightened because the interviewer's eyes, fixed to his/her writing, misses facial contact and other non-verbal referencing that together help to tune the meanings of spoken words. An interpretation that is heavily ear-dependent is likely to be very different from an interpretation employing the usual mix of senses.

If the interviewer manages to avoid cooption, then he/she may dominate. Note taking is an activity that can lend itself to massive infusions of the interviewer's own attitudes, interests, and needs. Unconsciously, as the fingers write, the interviewer may be grasping for the tightest control of the type and ordering of data. Improperly handled, notes become the coded instrument of a dominant interviewer and the respondent's case becomes perverted to fulfil the interviewer's goals. In terms of the three styles of evaluation posited by MacDonald (1976), bureaucratic, autocratic, and democratic, note taking would always seem more naturally suited to the former two. In the latter case, the most stringent discipline is needed in order to come near to upholding a democratic intent.

A major concern in note taking is the sheer loss of hard information. There is inevitable reductionism in its use. Babies may be thrown out with bath water, underlying threads missed, and facts mislaid. Because it tends to focus on the highlights of the respondent's case, background detail, contextual evidence, and powerful, though illogical or not immediately apparent influences may be omitted as extraneous noise. Data that depend entirely upon note recordings will remain questionable until the quality of the writer can be vouchsafed.

A last problematic area is the lack of leverage that notes afford in presenting cases. Because they can always be called into question as 'mere interpretation', they do not represent a means by which an interviewer can hold a respondent to witness in the development of his or her case. Without the actual words, what is there to barter with? The undoubted consequence of this lack of hard currency or notes to provide ample evidence of the interviewee's public status rather than his/her personal understandings.

Generating, Processing and Reporting Interview Data: Two Profiles

I have argued that it is a mistake to assume that techniques of recording are so malleable and adaptive that they can be harnessed to any intent. Different techniques make different processes and products possible.

The organizational rationale of research methodology artificially distinguishes between data generation, data processing, and data reporting, dealing with each as a separate, though not always separable, phase of interviewing practice. Of course, this is not the case. It is only a linear construct and an arbitrary, mechanistic way of severing a whole process into parts. Data analysis permeates everything we do as researchers and evaluators (Sanger, 1995a). Following the earlier argument that interviews need to be penetrative, fair, and valid, MacDonald and I used the criteria of effectiveness, fairness, and validity to examine the claims made for each practice at each stage of the operation. Finally, we used the columns of the tables to separate the formal properties of the interviews from the claims and criticisms we thought were associable with them.

The result was a highly condensed but, we hoped, not impenetrable description of two approaches to the unstructured interview. We wanted to make it possible for the reader not just to compare and contrast the approaches but to reconstruct the realities they attempted to represent. No profile is offered of an approach to interviewing that combines both recording techniques. It was argued that duplication of technique could mitigate weaknesses in the original paper, but the strength of counter arguments based on the compounding of constraints, mutually exclusive benefits, or simply the labour intensity of such an approach was suggested to explain why interviewers choose one or the other. That such a choice has consequences for the nature of the data itself, is what was established. I now hold the view that a mixed media approach is essential. I err, as I did then, towards note taking in preference to taping but I **use** data I generate far more as an artefact of our times than a representation of social and political realities. Of course, at one level, the data becomes necessary to acquit myself in research in the exemplary ways that funding agencies require. But at other levels, the levels which provide meta-views, perhaps, I feel less inclined to stay with the confines of the data but to use them as the means to probe the cultural contexts which help generate them.

Note taking is the traditional tool of many fields of research and has, consequently, become strongly associated with the researcher's freedom to investigate, analyze and theorize. Time and usage have largely conspired to reduce the debate over its appropriateness. Tape recording, on the other hand, is by comparison, a relative upstart. Its inception in research was, and still is, attended by misgivings over the ethics of surveillance its appropriateness, and its sensitivity. Any attempt to compare and contrast their virtues in relation to effectiveness, fairness, and validity, do so within the boundary of an overall concern for the democratizing influences each may have upon research or evaluation. As may be gathered from what I have said above, I begin to wonder whether these apparently lucid and admirable concerns are misplaced. Whether they leave us imprisoned in past rhetoric, a rhetoric which pervades our acts in ways that constrain us in acts of conservation of social orders and relations which actually maintain inequality and injustice rather than oppose them.

In this context there is an interesting dichotomy between some of the leading exponents of each recording technique. Whereas notes have, in themselves, are not evidenced in a strong and consistent model of practice and the ethics of note taking appear to be rewritten by each researcher, in tape recording, if the interests of respondents are to be upheld, certain principles and practices seem to be required. In many ways, exploiting the properties of the tape to mitigate the dangers of misrepresentation ensures a certain democratic procedure. It would seem that whereas for the democratic model, principles and procedures create an actively participative constituency and a restraint of academic or bureaucratic usurpation (as much a constraint upon the interviewer as anyone else), within note taking democracy resides in the intent or otherwise of the interviewer.

We have then divergent political forms, one in which the interviewer assumes personal responsibility for the integrity, validity and appropriateness of the account and one in which the interviewer, faced with this problem, tries to devolve some of that responsibility upon all the constituency members of the research population because it provides complete texts of participant accounts that remain as objective data throughout the programme or project to their completion and beyond. It remains a protection and defence for each participant and enables him/her to assume first-person, direct-action status within the research or evaluation activity. Thus the possibility of researcher and evaluator control appears to be restricted. But is it merely delayed? Does the stage-by-stage transfer of power from interviewee to interviewer maximally disadvantage the respondents. In this sense the whole procedure can be seen as a flytrap of the patient spider. Notes, on the other hand, produce a more complex infusion of interviewer influence. Decisions cannot be delayed but are the stuff of transaction. Note taking is a continuous process of synthetic transformation and must always face major problems of systematic error and bias.

Lou Smith, a note taker, approaches these pitfalls by invoking the collected viewpoints of insider groups and individuals as safeguards against a hardening and monolithic interpretation of the case. However, these viewpoints, these diverse rationales, are not kept in their intact syntactical forms by the note taker but require 'attending and conceptualising styles similar to those audience uses' (Smith, 1981). Here is one way in which note taking may shape the language of reporting. A note taker is more likely to think in terms of 'vicarious experience' and 'false consciousness' than a tape recordist, because such terms are part of the genre of research literature. A tape recordist need only say, 'Attend to the actual words'. Literary forms and devices provide a number of useful guidelines for the note taker. Take Smith's description of the overall product: 'Eventually we have an outline which holds. It has a structure reflecting three major dimensions: integrity, complexity and creativity. By integrity I mean it has a theme, a thesis, a point of view.' And he goes on to compare the development of an evaluation with that of a picture, poem, or novel, which 'seems to develop something of a life of its own'.

While the same pressures are on the tape recorder user to find communicable forms, he/she has fewer options if he/she is committed to preserving the epistemologies (political structures) of respondents. The tape recorder user's prime concern is exploring live evidence with the reader. He/she must hold to heterogeneity. Thus the natural outcome of the tape is theatre (Tom Stoppard: 'Writing plays is the only respectable way you can contradict yourself in public.') But notes, while wishing for similar outcomes, have the added complication of providing a product in a traditional narrative form that must uphold its integrity through the quality of its language. Like it or not, the pressure is on the evaluator or researcher to tell a good, coherent story. At the negotiation phase of ethical research or evaluation, what is negotiated by the note taker must invite, implicitly, an approval of narrative quality and style. In all but the final stage of negotiation of tape-based extracts, there are no such features to tax the respondent. He/she is asked to authenticate live data. The respondent retains control over a unitary form. In final drafts the literacy confusions remain for the note-taken summary of summaries, but it is only at this stage that tape-based accounts become as perplexing for the negotiating respondent. Now, a text is supplied in which the respondent's words are embedded, displayed in an arrangement, with the words of others in a form whose meaning for and impact upon an audience is extremely difficult to judge. In both cases final drafts are, as often as not, faits accomplis of form and substance that may do little to deliver the original promises of respondent control.

Despite their more overt denial of democratic process, note-based accounts conform to the expectations of literate audiences in a way that the more documentary forms suggested by tapes do not. For naturalism read narrative imperative. Style seduces. We all want to be part of a good story. The writer retains favour through literary largesse.

On a more practical level, the interviewer is often part of a team or, if working alone, he/she may have adopted a plan of action that requires feedback and advice to a project. Lou Smith writes about sitting with the rest of the team and brainstorming, using read-out notes as a stimulus to provide a profile of a program. Notes here can be seen as relatively frictionless compared with tapes. Tapes are caught in time-locked confidentiality until the process of transcription and negotiated use have been completed. In any case they take a lot of listening to and are not easy to skim. Tapes lack the flexibility of use that makes notes attractive. Notes remain the best communication device within the action of a program. Exactly *what* is communicated and its ad hoc validity, is what is at question.

Glaser and Strauss (1967) in their grounded theory work, defend the investigator's right to 'analyze his data and decide(s) what data to collect next and where to find them, in order to develop his theory, as it emerges'. We have a sense here of what Smith (1981) following Malinowski, means by extolling foreshadowing in preference to preconceiving in naturalistic evaluation. The task is more daunting for the note keeper than the tape user. Note-taken interviews have necessarily a greater interrogative edge and a greater reliance on what is already known (conceptualized). The need for concise mnemonics on paper and the requirement for progressive refinement in the interests of the final synthesis increases the chances of slippage from foreshadowing to preconceiving. In comparison, the very obduracy of tapes in terms of processing and the respondents' control over them together delay the researcher or evaluator's ability to get on with discovering and organizing emergent issues and establishing priorities.

There are no absolute distinctions in the nature and quality of interviews based on different recording techniques. The influence of interviewer values and intentions is such that the distinctions become blurred with greater skill and experience. Nor would there be an implication that an inescapable partition between research and evaluations resulting from use of one or the other technique, leading to totally distinct accounts. But, at different stages in the conduct and use of interviews, each technique has sufficient inherent idiosyncrasy for it to constrain or enhance what interviewer are trying to accomplish. The complexion of the whole enquiry may be affected by the choice of recording technique.

Postscript

Here are brief examples to illustrate differences in form and content of interviews involving note taking, tape recording and a combination of the two. They come from recent projects at the Centre for Applied Research in Management Education and Training.

Note Taking

The TV is on when I arrive at about 3.40 pm.

Ashleigh is sitting on the floor watching and younger brother Spencer is sitting in a big armchair watching. Mum takes me into the sitting room where the children are and we sit down but the TV is left on and the volume is not turned down.

I ask what sort of equipment they have in the house. Mum says that they have a video, hi-fi and a TV — all kept in the sitting room. There is also a TV in the kitchen but this does not work any more and they have not got around to seeing what's wrong with it yet. Each of the two children has a walkman and a radio. Spencer has a TV in his room and a Sega Mastersystem. Ashleigh has not got a TV but does have a Mastersystem. (*Screen Based Entertainment Technology and the Young Learner*, British Library and British Film Institute, 1994–96)

Tape Recording

(Int. = Interviewer; Res. = respondent)
Int: Has anyone talked to you about starting before this?
Res: I think my mum told me.

Int: Can you remember what she said, the words she used?
Res: I think she said when you — when two people love each other, I think she said you go to bed and do it, then you have children.
Int: Did she talk about periods and why you have them?
Res: I think she said the egg breaks away and then the egg — oh is it the ovary breaks away then it fills up again like a tank, then it stays like it for another month.

(*Evaluation of Sexual Health Education for People With Learning Difficulties*, East Norfolk Health Commission, 1995)

A Tape and Notes Combination

I ask if there had only been one computer in the house. They had apparently originally had a Master system but that had got broken. They then got the Nintendo which they had for about seven months before mum sold it. Scott then shouts out that they also used to have a Gameboy. Mum says that this has also gone now because it got broken. Scott shouts out 'Yeah, that was me. I used to keep head-butting it.' Mum says 'Yes, that's his temper again.'

I ask exactly what happened and mum explains that he got cross because the game was not going well and then more in fun than anything else, he bashed it on his head and it just broke'. She giggled a bit when she said this and Scott laughed — his friend started to laugh too. I ask if mum consulted Scott before selling the Nintendo. 'No, I just decided and then went straight ahead. I knew I'd get grief over it so I just did it. He used to get up at 6.00 in the morning and would stay on it until midnight if he could. Wouldn't you?' (to Scott) 'Yeah, definitely.' (*Screen Based Entertainment Technology and the Young Learner*, British Library and British Film Institute, 1994–96)

The three pieces of text are different in style and content and each provides a different kind of information to the researcher. Each has been used within the process of analysis. Is it my preoccupation with literary forms which makes the last example most redolent of the interview? Is it the very narrative drive, the descriptive language, the very novelish look of it, that appeals and convinces me? Is it less easy to manipulate than the first two forms? Has it an entirety which makes it difficult to break up? Am I, as Derrida would aver, a victim of the persuasion of the author that what she has seen is accurately conveyed?

8   Research in the Technological Sense

Maybe the fly isn't sick at all. Maybe he's trying to ask you a question.

Technological mediation rules our lives. The blood and guts realities of our forebears are being erased by the virtual realities of our moving image makers, our sound recordists, our photographers, our illusionists. Our experience of the world is increasingly mediated by the cold dispassionate technologies of fibre optics, silicon, lasers, CD ROM. We will shop for groceries or take a walk through a museum by flicking switches in the front room and inserting our smart cards. We are extending our presence over time and distance via the huge, ungovernable networks of communication. It is not surprising that research is embracing this world. How it does so will become a central issue in research ethics. The debate between quantification and naturalistic approaches has often hinged upon the degree to which the former dehumanizes the realities lived by respondents. One can imagine virtual futures where this is taken to the extreme. Already, programs exist which project scenarios of devastation for military planners, three-dimensional building plans under seismic shock for architects and patients' cancerous bodies for surgeons. One can foresee research using similar computer modelling devices to pilot new products, predict changes to the environment, project public attitudes to new laws or evaluate policy on practice. Whole populations of ghosts will exist within machines, with their biographies created to emphasize individuality and difference, homogeneity, class, ethnicity and gender. These zombies categorized as ersatz communities will be bought and sold according to their apparent effectiveness in modelling the population 'out there'. Meanwhile the population 'out there' will emulate, act out and wilfully mimic the ghosts presented to it through the media and over time the gap between real and machine will close, disturbingly. It is argued by some (for example, Docker, 1994) that the media can only exist within an arena involving audience participation, either directly, as in game shows, studio debates or indirectly through popularity of serial melodramas, sport and so on. However, a more caustic view of such phenomena would suggest that *participation*, itself, as a real-time descriptor of lived reality is undergoing metamorphosis. Inexorably, we are learning the process of mediated participation. Virtual participation is just around the tv tube.

Whilst discussing more prosaic matters, in what follows, it is important to remember that the present controls we have over technology will be eroded by its new sophistication, as time passes.

Electronic Ears

In chapter 6 I discussed the use of tape recording in interviews. I won't dwell too much more upon the use of audio tape, save to say that small machines with microcassettes are very accurate for transcriptions, if used properly. A couple of pointers. Ethically — and acoustically — place the recorder next to the individual, during interviews, out of eye line. Explain the workings of the machine and encourage the interviewee to use the pause button. Suggest that at any time s/he can stop the recording. Giving power over technology helps to put the respondent at ease.

As far as group work is concerned, in classroom or board meeting, always use a stereo recorder. In playing back you will see why. In stereo you create a field of sound and can differentiate voices and positions in relation to the microphone. The more sophisticated the technology of sound recording, the better the result — but, sometimes, there is an increased interference in the naturalness of the setting. Sound mikes combined with video or cassette recorders obviously take more setting up and are relatively foreign to most people's experience whilst the ubiquitous walkman has made the cassette recorder familiar and relatively unthreatening. In what follows, sound is as important as image.

Electronic Eyes

The camera first shows us the entire body; we then expect it to track forward slowly into fascinating detail, the bloody sockets of the missing eyes. But Hitchcock gives us an inversion of the process we expect: instead of slowing down, he drastically speeds up, with two abrupt cuts, each bringing us closer to the subject, he quickly shows us the corpse's head. (Zizek, 1991, p. 93)

Videotaping has become a commonplace in research, staff development, appraisal, teaching and learning. However, each of these arenas of use makes different demands on the technology. Research has specific needs — the production of accessible data. The dos and don'ts of videotaping for research can be boiled down to a simple maxim:

'Make Sure It's on the Screen, can be Heard and can be Seen'

This means that if the researcher is not behind the camera, instructions to the operator must be exact and unequivocal. Rather like minimalist writing a la Robbes Grillet, all the embellishments of Hitchock or Ford must be eschewed. No pans around the group, no close ups. Aim for a fixed position, fixed focus, wherever possible. Mount the camera, decide on what's to be in the frame and leave the whole thing running. Only in tracking shots, such as engaging in pupil pursuit, do you break the rule.

The reason is this. It is astonishing how, as operators of the technology, we slip into unconscious editing-by-selection. We define what's on the screen, unwittingly allowing our biases and interests to dominate. Later, when we come to try to interpret and analyze the images, we find a host of alternative threads of interest leading off screen and beyond our recall. I have had occasion to use a young male operator, only to discover that the group of students being photographed appears to be all female. An equal number of males had virtually vanished, as he used the camera to home-in, exclusively, on his subjects.

The following section looks at what may be a productive avenue for video-based research. This involves content analysis of words spoken and the semiotics of body language. Given the current emphasis on professional processes as opposed to outcomes or products, the ways that professionals conduct themselves in libraries, classrooms, wards and shop floors, the focus on more traditional areas of content has diminished. Process dominates product. McLuhan rules. The medium is the message. The processes of teaching are all. In trying to discover the affective and cognitive understandings of students in classrooms, for example, modern enquiry tends either to interview or video record participants in action, following this with attempts to seek out their self-conscious articulation of what is happening in their environment. This has always been a fraught business. By focusing attention on the areas in which the researcher has a particular interest, participants may or may not respond authentically. They may not *know why they do things*. Most classrooms do not and can not afford the time for discursive forays into pupil or student-led critical discourse which might train them in such articulation. The development of meta-views of reality are part of curriculum innovation still. So what happens when the voices of students, concerning their everyday reality, is denied institutional majorities?

What follows is a partial case study of a single lesson. It is partial because it concentrates not only upon one feature of a lesson, the language uttered by the pupils, but because it focuses upon a particular aspect of that language.

There is always a deceitful aspect to the reconstruction and analysis of classroom events. The written is always a fragmentary representation of what actually happens. In this chapter, the events described were only made available to this observer second hand on a video-tape. I first saw the tape in Victoria University, Canada, another culture, whilst teaching research methods to masters and doctoral students. The class depicted on the video-tape are part of a programme for 'gifted' pupils. It is a mixed gender group of 13 and 14-year-olds. The classroom is traditionally organized, with teacher, teacher's desk and blackboard facing the class. The subject is philosophy. Now, as you, the reader are making sense of the context, think now of the teacher, Bernie Bowker, having the class read part of the transcript of a play, which is to act as a stimulus for discussion. The play chosen is full of its own Laingian knots. This, together with the ensuing discussion, in turn becomes the video tape. The tape acts as data for a masters group of researchers in Canada, involving them in critical discussion of classroom observation techniques. The audio version of that tape acts as a source for a paper written later in England. Here follows *one* break-down of the pattern of events as shown on the video-tape. (Most of us would assume that there are many possible summaries and other constructions to be put on such complex events.)

Minutes	Activities
5	Play reading involving pupils in pairs plus a narrator. In it the child asks a father about the nature of questioning. Bernie changes who will read the parts from time to time.
?	A length of time (a few minutes, edited out of the video) where the class have to draw up questions on the text that they wish to be to have debated)
5	Their questions are written by fellow pupils on the board and Bernie asks them to look for patterns among them in order to cluster the questions and synthesize them. These new major questions will focus the debate.
25	Bernie asks the class which of the clusters they would like to discuss. first. A girl suggests 'the sick fly'. There is general agreement to this. What follows is the discussion.

Glancing down this outline of the session, few educationalists would see anything unusual about the structure of the lesson as an epitome of classroom debate. Certainly, it has traditional overtones. The teacher controls the direction of discussion and the vast proportion of it is mediated through him. After all, he is modelling for them the protocols of *philosophical debate*. An example:

> (Bernie examines the blackboard, now full of suggested topics for philosophical discussion.)
> *Bernie*: What subject would you like to discuss first? Which one? Er . . . Christine?
> *Christine*: The sick fly.
> *Bernie*: You'd like to discuss the sick fly. All right, how many would like to discuss it? We're going to discuss them all. (Hands go up.) Right, let's begin with the sick fly, then.

What Bernie does is emphasize how the group should use language in debate and the logical basis and courtesies of philosophical discussion. We could look at the transcript at length and see that he maintains a strong grip on proceedings, sharing out the discussion amongst his pupils, highlighting their rights — even to being bizarre in a response or to holding an unusual viewpoint. He is always there, chivvying, sharing, illuminating, appealing to knowledge. From the point of view of an induction into philosophical debate, the session can be seen to be a great success.

But, like all lessons the session has much more to it than its face value structure and function, realised here as putative philosophical discourse. It is at another level of structure and function that I'd like to explore the contents of the video. First, I'd like to describe the hypothesis which arose in my mind on my first viewing of the videotape — and the context for its appearance.

Whilst asking the group of teachers, including Bernie, to adopt strategies for observing and then analyzing the video, I wanted to throw in a less predictable approach which would help to destabilize my, and the group's, assumptions about what was happening before us on the television screen. In this I felt, as does Lacan (Ulmer, 1985), that the more we are experienced and know about our discipline, the more we rely upon set strategy and pre-digested material: Pedagogy needs to be allied to invention. I foresaw that they would produce a range of strategies (checklists, vignettes, counts, dramatic highlights, language analysis etc.) *which would confirm what we assumed was happening*. That is, that here was an excellent example of teacher-directed debate, with apparent benefits for pupils and apparently not deleterious to the relationship between teacher and pupils. We would be transfixed by the medium (process) and not the message (content). For after all, wasn't my masters course underpinned by the thesis that teaching is about process rather than content?

So I looked at the frozen content of the video recording and am reminded now of some lines in *The Illusion of the End* by Baudrillard. (1994):

> When ice freezes, all excrement rises to the surface. And so, when the dialectic was frozen, all the sacred excrement of the dialectic came to the surface. (p. 26)

The poetic image of a sick fly, with its many literary and film connotations from Blake to Cronenberg, caught my immediate attention. I began to note the words and images which seemed linked to the metaphor of the sick fly. Here are some of them:

> fly, sick, die, unnatural causes, old age, sickness, disease, heart attack, shot, Aunt and Dad dropped dead, virus, bacteria, foreign, injury, afflicted, germ warfare, skin, infection, ill, vomiting, nauseous, disgusting, insane, heart disease, alien, fester, blood, germs, carriers, haemophiliacs, hospitals, stick a knife into Marie.

Once I began to do it I had a strange sensation of being privy to another world. To lifting a stone. The session was redolent of a pupil-group's fixation with some of the darker and less handleable aspects of life. In many ways, the lesson was a tour de force. Here were a group totally involved in philosophic debate. Obeying the rules, carrying out the role of learners within the strict parameters laid down by the teacher. However, when I pointed out to this teacher research group my own findings, there was a strange silence. No-one had noticed this overriding aspect of content. And now it was pointed cut, no-one *could see the value of knowing it!*

Why were we blind to the information and its consequences? Was there something here that could tell us a great deal about learning in classrooms? And a way of researching it?

The Kingdom of the Blind

For anyone engaged in developing teachers' awareness of classroom processes, the reasons why we were blind may be more obvious. To begin with certain ways of structuring classrooms have become vogue in the last couple of decades. And with these structures there have been concomitant kinds of questions which have come to dominate our enquiries. Whether using Flanders type grids or checklists or methods of narrative portrayal, a bi-polar tension has manifested itself in goal setting and, therefore, the way that we observe phenomena. This usually polarizes as didactic v. interactive, democratic v. authoritarian and teacher-centred v. student-centred and leads to a pursuit of classroom detail which tries to establish where the teacher is positioned between the poles of the spectrum. The result is a whole deluge of classroom research which examines every aspect of teacher *performance* and pupil *participation* in classroom life. The tendency is to tease out the implicit and explicit rules of engagement, the strategies, the roles and the language, using a logic which begins with these reductionist polarities.

My present interest in how classrooms come to be (mis)understood by these approaches is tied to the hypothesis that curriculum development only comes about alongside teacher development. Change teachers' views of their own potential and they are more likely to innovate and change the curriculum. The present vogue in challenging teachers' views is by directing interest towards the processes of teaching. And along the way the content of teaching is severed from the process and becomes assumed to be a less significant backdrop of the teacher-learner relationship. This is overstating the case but it is an important aspect of present educational myth making. The clichés 'a good teacher can teach anything' or 'a subject is often taught better when the teacher is a page ahead of the pupil' are examples.

Now I am not arguing a back to 'products' or 'content' curriculum. The point being made is that current practice in education is driving us to study classrooms in such a way as to do damage to the integrity of the field of study.

Content cannot be separated from process. We are asking questions concerning 'how' and 'why' statements are made in classrooms but we have, of late, shied away from analyzing 'what' the statements mean, We need to know what is being communicated at an explicit and implicit level.

I'm not talking here about teachers', pupils' and students' articulated views of teachers, learning, peers or the institution. Today that's okay. I'm speaking about the classroom talk under the direction of the teacher; the talk that is acceptable to the teacher as subject-related and part of the syllabus. The public talk. The kind of talk that would get pupils marks if they were being orally assessed. It is precisely because it is part of classroom life and signifies that the syllabus is being covered that we become blind to its potential as a vehicle for highly charged classroom discourse — and a reservoir of insights for understanding human interaction in classrooms.

Under the Surface

Before we forget the immediate context, let us return to the audio-tape. The agenda of the sick fly has been agreed, according to the protocols Bernie Bowker has laid down. Discourse develops, regulated by Bernie. The pupils need little stimulus. They maintain a high level of interaction. Bernie is the philosopher-policeman, keeping them to the rules of the road of discourse. Here is an example of the way they discuss . . .

Bernie: So it isn't something about which we can debate. They either get sick or . . . ?

Voices They die . . .

Bernie: (ignoring or not hearing) . . . or they don't get sick before they die. Yes Franz?

Franz: I think they do get sick because . . . if you die that is . . . if you die of old age that is getting sick isn't it? If you're getting sick you're gonna die.

Bernie: (Interrupting voices) Franz made a statement, would you say it again about 'if you die . . .'

Franz: If you die isn't that being sick? You have to be sick to die of natural causes.

Bernie: OK, well, that's an interesting question. It may be relevant to this scientific question (points to board). Adrian?

Adrian: I think that er . . . dying of old age can be considered as a sickness because my Mum always says that when you get old its like a sickness. But its a disease you cannot cure. But it could be considered as a sickness.

Bernie: OK, Karen?

Karen: Well I wouldn't consider it as a sickness because you get old and die. It's just like dying . . . naturally. But say you die of a heart attack — that, I would consider, sick. If you died naturally I wouldn't consider it sick.

What seems striking about this debate is its orderliness, its acquiescence to teacher control, the complexity of insights and the challenge to the pupil. But that is the surface. Is there anything happening underneath which we ought to ask about? Already the subject matter has been noted. Pupils have chosen to discuss this topic and go about it with zest. However, almost immediately, via Franz, the fly becomes transposed to the universal 'you'. Fly becomes human. It is the human condition of mortality that is centre stage. Within the context of the accepted agenda of the debate, major questions are emerging. And it's not just mortality, its the practical reality of the nastiness which attends it (look back to the original list of words and images used by the pupils in the session.) Why? The answer may be in the nature of metaphor. What we are encountering is discourse at different levels. Barthes (1984) refers to Benveniste's proposition that meaning can be distributed across a horizontal plane of one level or it can be integrated vertically through levels.

> To understand a narrative is not merely to follow the unfolding of the story, it is also to understand its construction in 'stories', to project the horizontal concatenations of the narrative 'thread' on to an implicitly vertical axis. (p. 87)

Reading the text of classroom interaction often seduces the researcher into an apparent world of narrative. The desire to tell a story, to make unities of fragmented discourse, grip us in our modernist drives. Thus, there are similarities with detective fiction. Whilst it is impossible to render the continuum of life, as experienced by any one individual, in script, there is a continuous search for a literary form to express it.

> There is a certain self-reflexive strain in the detective novel; it is a story of the detective's efforts to tell the story, i.e. to reconstitute what 'really happened' around and before the murder, and the novel is finished not when we get to the answer to 'Whodunnit?' but when the detective is finally able to tell the 'real story' in the form of the linear narrative. (Zizek, 1991, p. 49)

Researchers are like detectives. But like all the great detective figures, good researchers are driven to providing more than the superficially observable. Understanding becomes distributed at the level of observation and cutting through that level is the vertical axis of theory. For the detective this means seeking out *motive*. For the researcher we substitute *meaning*. Gathering data amounts to gathering the observable or staying at the level of *form*. We intersect this plane with our interpretations. But the evidence from Bernie Bowker's class is that there are even observable phenomena which we fail to see. And the fact that we don't see them is because they contain elusive levels of meaning.

We can analyze how content may act as a vehicle for these two levels of communication and what these levels represent.

Two-faced Communication

We have rehearsed well enough what the superficial level of communication is in Bernie Bowker's lesson. It is the achievement of public or institutional respectability according to the conventions of a particular segment of Canadian education, the promotion of giftedness. In short, the pupils and the teacher are playing by publicly articulated rules. However, the underbelly of this level seems to be working through antithesis. It is telling an opposing story a story which goes something like this. . . .

> We are gifted kids. This is our significance. We are the best around. We are the healthy ones. We do philosophy to exercise our minds. It is rule-bound. The conventions of the classroom are rule-bound. We are encouraged by our teacher to think freely about any subject but the one freedom which is denied us is freedom from the classroom. Our freedoms are framed within the classroom context. Our taboo is one which does not allow critique of schooling. So when we come to discuss openly some subject we inject a critique of schooling into it so it hardly shows, yet we can come away with some feeling of challenging the taboo. We take the subject matter and choose sickness and disease which are social taboos. These, the young mind is not supposed to consider in schooling, as they are regarded as morbid and unhealthy: the antithesis of health, the dark converse world to our own. By doing so we point up our role in schooling. Our own limitations. We also point up the diseases of schooling, our rules and roles, which load us down. Just as natural death can be seen as a disease, so can 'natural' underachievement — the state in which the non-gifted find themselves. In this free (sic) discourse we maintain our own agenda whilst playing the game. In the classroom of doxa, we must operate by paradox.

Gordon et al (1980) notes that Foucault sees discourse as actualizing the multiple strategies of power whilst overseeing their application. In this case discourse oversees the lack of power in pupil discourse. The above summary is not meant to represent the views of the pupils in the class, it is meant to represent the power of metaphor within discourse and the levels which can be represented, either consciously or unconsciously, by the participants.

Given that discourse is fettered in classrooms by an expectation of convention, one which upholds the cognitive over the affective, it is not surprising that evidence of this particular class points up the fact that the affective must be driven somewhere. It can be found in the two-faced metaphor. The public face carrying the cognitive, acceptable logics of communication whilst the private face carries the chaotic, anarchic and repressed critiques of public. In short, critique of schooling is squeezed out of the domain of classroom discourse so that the pupils' affective responses are forced: into the ambiguous half-lit world of metaphoric communication . . .

Marie:	Getting back to the sick fly issue. If you were insane you would be considered sick.
Bernie:	Uhuh
Marie:	Flies go insane therefore I would say that they are sick. (Lots of voices) If you have ever seen a fly at a window sill, the fly just knows that it can't get through the glass. He keeps throwing himself against the window sill in any case.
Bernie:	Bernadette?
Bernadette:	How does the fly know he can't get through the glass?
Marie:	He's done it before. (Loud voices. Bernie shouts 'Hold it!')
Bernie:	Any statement made in this class is legitimate as long as it doesn't include obscenities. So, if Marie wants to make that statement, you accept that statement. You don't have to agree with it but I don't want any . . . negative response . . .

Here feeling has precedence over verbal articulation and language contains, unheard, the inarticulate, unconscious vehicle for critique. Like the Easter Island heads . . . what were assumed to be heads without bodies, are in fact vast torsos, now underground . . . the language of pupils has a submerged side which carries their attempts to analyze and understand but it remains largely unacknowledged. The metaphor is one of entrapment, of repeated attempts to break free and of insanity in the fly (a creature without premeditation). Though there are voices raised against Marie's analogy, it should not delimit the power of the discourse which is convened between and among voices. The pupils create an implicated debate, full of false trails, confusions and sudden leaps. It is a perfect example of Derrida's thesis that ordinary language defies categorisation and systematization (Ulmer, 1985). Concerning himself/herself with symbolic material will no doubt cause the classroom observer a whole host of rational problems!

Just as the proscenium arch must be abandoned (deconstructed) so that we can understand the dramaturgical construction of traditional theatre, the formal aspects of language of the classroom need stripping away before we can understand the other layers of meaning it may contain. Derrida and Pautrat (see *ibid*) argue that the deconstruction of the classroom exposes the authority of the teacher and his/her subservience to the structures of political power. Analysis of the language of pupils, whilst apparently gainfully employed in learning, may help to prove this to be so.

This is merely a preliminary attempt to look at language in classrooms in another light, one that is less dependent upon explicit or formal attributes and seeks to understand hidden codes of meaning. We can complete the exercise with some further examples from the classroom.

Bernie: Are we talking about two different things or the same thing. You're saying that if you get shot you believe that that's a sickness. It seems to me that we have a different word for that kind of event other than sickness. If we get cut or shot or . . . something like that, do we call that a sickness?

Voices: No! An accident! An injury!

Bernie: An injury! Is there a difference between an injury and a sickness? Jason?

Jason: To begin with I think we should define sick.

Bernie: Alright — define it.

Jason: When your body is . . . is . . . er . . .

Bernie: Anybody help him?

Girl: It's when you have a disease or virus in your body . . .

Bernie: So when your body is inhabited by a virus or bacteria that's foreign to it?

Voices: Yeah . . .

In this preoccupation with the differences between sickness and injury, there is a metaphoric possibility that freedom is again being addressed. They are evidently discriminating between what is the result of explicit acts and what results from the insidious penetration of the self. The former may be seen to be the laws or rules of everyday living whilst the latter could well refer to culture — or the social construction of reality. For 'gifted' pupils, motoring in debate, the metaphoric may take them further, emotionally, than the attempt to reason out a philosophic thesis.

Kate: We said injury is when someone does something to you and disease is when you've got something in your body making you uncomfortable and this usually lasts longer.

Bernie: Alright, Russell?

Russell: Well injury also includes when you do something to yourself . . . or also . . . like . . . if I were to hit . . . stick a knife into Marie — I'm . . . not sure I'd want to — but . . .

Marie: Yes he would!

Russell: That would be an injury to her but if she were to stick a knife into herself . . . that would also be an injury to her.

The ultimate oppression of constrictive schooling is the combination of social laws which are exemplified within it. As in the film *If*, the system creates such bottlenecks in emotional and intellectual development that the mind dwells on the most extreme response to this order. A condition Sartre has explored in novel and tract.

I'd like to finish by suggesting where this leads me in classroom and other group enquiry. It reaffirms the need to explore the processes of individuation within the extraordinary walls of schooling and the effects on learning of a straitjacketed affective climate. It pushes me to want to look at language as a multidimensional way of playing by imposed rules whilst subverting or critically examining them in covert metaphoric ways. From a pedagogical point of view, it suggests that the teacher should be required to open up the authority structures within institutional life to the debate of the institutional majority — pupils.

Having said that — the analysis which leads to these suggestions is highly personal. What makes this form of content analysis exciting is that the teacher could take the same data and weave another structure around it — one which would require testing over time and through the explicit and the implicit. It might be the taboo of death and disease, it might be the repression of sexuality or it might be the lack of spiritual nourishment. What it does allow is for the teacher to be inventive with his/her theories and thereby rekindle interest in the world beneath the surface of classrooms. A more productive discourse may well result from it.

9   Seven Types of Creativity: Observation And Data Analysis*

> It may be said that the business of analysis is to progress from poetical to prosaic, from intuitive to intellectual knowledge; evidently these are just the same sort of opposites, in that each assumes the other is also there. (William Empson (1930), *Seven Types of Ambiguity*)

One of the more provocative British Educational Research Association debates at the University of Stirling in 1992 took place in the symposium concerning qualitative data analysis. Its substance revolved around the messy world of qualitative research. Contributors such as Hammersley, Burgess and Rudduck aired in public some of their concerns with grounded theory approaches to research. Judging by the effect on some of the audience, it was unsettling in the extreme.

Among the speakers there were those who admitted that they retreated from grounded theory into forms of hypothetico deductive logic when the going became too desperate. That quantification provided answers, at least to the problem of satisfying the funding agency, when qualitative data had seemed to provide a permanent regression of questions. There was a starting account of wholesale confirmatory qualitative data from East Germany, which subsequently amounted to an entire teaching profession's conspiratorial lie. And, for this author, the emergence of a theme which continues to seep into the debate concerning data analysis but which is rarely admitted as a major issue. What was intimated was that the difference between hack research and research which might make a difference to its field of understanding, or its immediate audiences of actors, often resulted from the imagination of the researcher. Not from the painstaking reordering of indisputable facts but from the creative mind. This, it was felt, might be true equally for the quantifier and the naturalistic enquirer.

This invocation of the 'research imagination' has striking resemblances to explanations of other mysterious cognitive process which the skills and competencies curriculum cannot tie down in materialistic or behaviouristic language. Those aspects of teaching and learning which, in their implicit ways,

---

* This chapter is based on an article whose reference is: Sanger, J. (1994) 'Seven types of creativity', *BERA Journal*, **20**, 2.

transform individuals in the classroom and work place but defy theory and even, sometimes, speculation. It was comforting to know that our leading researchers fall back upon something akin to the classical thesis of the muse, the divine effluvia, when self-analysis fails to secure for them a theory of what constitutes quality in data analysis. Nor is this intended to be cynical or satirical. Text books rarely contain accurate accounts of how little is research in utterly systematic when it comes to transformative acts of data analysis.

Yet BERA symposia may be seen as living text books. Many come merely to learn, passively from their peers. Presentation as text is these days central to our pos-tmodern gatherings. Reception theory an explanatory form for audience engagement.

Why did people come to this particular symposium? Some because they wanted to know how to practice data analysis, utilizing grounded theory. A few because they wanted to be reassured that there weren't any certainties of approach. This impression was seemingly triangulated across individual paper sessions and other symposia. There were those who were desperate to know how things should be done and those who were happier having mud baths in the mire of ambiguity.

In many ways the problem is more typical of qualitative than quantitative research. When we hear the term 'qualitative', all the associations which tend to follow it like the trial of a snail, suggest ambiguity, compromise, pragmatism, Wittgensteinian games, subjectivity and relativity. It's often easier to attack and caricature the comatose body of positivism than to show how naturalistic enquiry is a breathing, authentic reality. So the question of how data analysis can be conducted, utilizing grounded theory approaches, foundered in the dialogue between those suburbanites wishing for order, street lamps, and the security of a pavement, and those ruralists, eschewing safety, who preferred the topography of the wild moors.

Imagination and Codification

Taking up some of the issues of that debate and relating it primarily to observation, this chapter examines the process of analysis. It is not assumed that analysis is a summative operation; that it happens at the end of intensive data gathering, a fitting together of the pieces as in detective fiction. Some researchers do it that way, of course, claiming that interpretations would be prefigured, otherwise. They claim that in the interests of neutrality, they avoid interpretation until the very end. Others take the opposing view that the researcher analyzes as s/he goes and is best served by making this formative interpretive process explicit. The former falls foul of the implicit theories and experiences within the researcher's biography which blinker or channel perception (Reichenbach, 1938). The latter commits the possible sin of a too premature justification of interpretations, leading to a mind-set which cannot see alternatives thereafter.

> **Immortal cells key to cancer**
>
> ... Now scientists are hunting for the 'engine of cell destruction', he said. A set of novel enzymes, proteolytic enzymes, has just been discovered by Junying Yuan of Boston University. They cause the cell to self-destruct. The enzymes have not been discovered before because scientists were not looking for them. (*The Times Higher Education Supplement*, 21 April 1995)

Whatever the approach, there are problems inherent in the way that data are utilized in explanatory accounts. Within research and evaluation projects data are categorized, schematized, patterned, weighed and prioritized into 'plausible stories' (the term used in the BERA symposium.) The continuing running battle between the scientistic view of research and the hermeneutical view of research spills out in any debate on the quality of data analysis. The greater the use of the imagination, it is contended, the less rigorous and valid the interpretation, the greater the use of strict patterning, according to well-developed and explicit criteria, the more valid the end findings. The opposing view is that highly interpretive accounts may be seen to be closer to the spirit of the times and the prevalent understandings under consideration. Strictly controlled attempts to codify and categorize the research process lead to stilted and lifeless renditions of the human condition.

Strauss and Corbin (1991) represent one end of the qualitative spectrum with a framework of careful and comprehensive codification. For them, data are broken down into categories and sub-categories which can then act as units for reformulation into new interpretations. At the other extreme, researchers such as Moustakis (1990), Winter (1986) and Walker (1982) operate much closer to research journalism. Here, the attempt is to maintain a holistic correlation between data and rendered account, either through phenomenological acts such as empathy or through the power of metaphor to portray more closely, likenesses.

We must accept at the outset that in analysis the optimum that can be achieved is partially prefigured by research design and research methods (Burgess, 1992). It would simplify greatly the coherency of this chapter to concentrate upon what happens after these phases, when you try to make sense of what you have gathered, whether on the day, or several days later when the mound has grown intimidatingly in the researcher's data store. But these relationships need exploring. Research remains a composite and interrelated set of activities, riddled with persistent ideological and epistemological assumptions.

The central question in research design and research methods, as far as their impact on analysis is concerned, relates to whether these aspects are seen to be causally connected to analysis or whether analysis is merely in a contingent relationship with them. In other words, if, as with Corbin and Strauss, grounded theory depends upon a set of logical relations between research conception and research outcomes, then analysis is already pre-figured within the process. The whole process may thus be akin to painting by Stanley Spencer, starting with the shapes drawn in and filling in the colour, later.

The less mechanistic the approach to design and data gathering, the more the data at the end of the day create coherency problems for the analyst. Keeping all the variables screened in maintains a holistic integrity in the data but presents the analyst with complex multi-dimensional possibilities which deny simple or linear explanations. A middle ground between these approaches utilises progressive focussing, whereby the boundaries of research are drawn wide at the outset and are then tightened, like a noose around what is imagined to be the significant neck of the data.

A question which arises here is the critical posture of the researcher. This determines the essential scepticism with which the data is regarded. Data can have levels of intrinsic significance to any researcher, depending upon theoretical leanings, personal needs or cultural imperatives. The question usually concerns representation. In other words, of what is the observational data a representation? Is it representative of every day reality, as might be found, for example, in an NVQ competency check list which assesses whether bricks are being laid correctly (Bhaskar, 1979)? Is it representative of the social, psychological and political forces which influence actors' beliefs and perceptions as in, say, accounts of discretionary policing of demonstrations (Habermas, 1974)? Or is it representative of an epistemic level beneath even the latter, the regulatory mechanisms which give rise to the language and concepts which help determine the way that actors and researchers separately and together, theorize in the first place (Foucault, 1974). Depending where you feel yourself to be on this spectrum will determine how you think of and use data. For the naturalistic enquirer it is usually enough to frame everyday reality, positing merely the perceptual understandings of actors within the case. For critical theorists, there is a need to determine the degree to which these actors are consigned to their perceptual fate, by developing social and political exegeses to explain their behaviours.

For the post-modernist language philosopher, data are arbitrary and are therefore vulnerable to a wide variety of analytical operations. The authorship of the data, in the form of actors' statements and non-verbal behaviours, may be denied and the entire process of data gathering together with the data itself, seen to be a composite artifact regulated by arbitrary historical currents. In this extreme view of data, even inter-subjective reality is an effect of epistemic underwriting. The value of such anarchic dissection remains, however, more philosophical than practical. Whatever the false consciousness, the blinkered conditioning, the passivity in the face of endemic cultural power conflicts, research in its applied forms remains substantially locked in the predicament of the everyday. At most, the underlying or inherent forces operating on, or within, individuals may be noted but it is to more prosaic relations between actors and action, that researchers are forced to turn in order to maintain their livelihood. Generally, researchers belong to the same construction of reality as those they are observing.

The debate between these views of data comes down, therefore, to the degree to which data are accepted as authentic indicators of life as lived. Eagleton (1983) puts it pithily, as follows:

> An interpretation upon which every one is likely to agree may be regarded as a fact.

Even accepting, at the extreme, that they are the outward signifiers of an arbitrary melee in which we struggle, creating meanings as we go, nevertheless they are all we have to convince others that we have been here. To some extent we have to remain within our frames of accepted behaviour, in order to survive. These may be seen to be active discourses a la Habermas, language games a la Wittgenstein or paradigms a la Kuhn.

Research for Action

The world of those we research needs to be re-presented by researchers to actors in accessible and recognizable forms. Researchers may then tug critically at the fabric of that reality with interpretation, recommendation, imported understandings, wider portrayals in which that reality is embedded, both historical and social and through the use of language, itself. The discourse in which actors are embedded when the researcher finds them, is disrupted by contagion with the research discourse — however that becomes manifest. If the gap between them is too great, the research discourse will be rejected or, worse still, remain inaccessible owing to its lack of familiar feature. In terms of research having the means to generate action, it must accept some of the conventions of its actors. Another way of expressing it is to say that it must obey, to a sufficient degree, the social constructs of the population being studied — the prevailing paradigm.

Because of rapid changes of philosophic outlooks this century, the present day consensual view of reality of the person in the street seems largely a mixture of prevailing scientism and a weak form of relativism. Research work, consequently, faces mixed demands for validity, relating it to objectivity and generalizability, whilst also requiring some evidence of plural viewpoints. Thus, qualitative research defends itself by invoking justificatory processes such as triangulation, mutuality, cultural agency, relatability, trustworthiness and reflexivity. Rupturing this context, in order for the light of new understanding to enter discourse, is the art of research. It is sometimes this process which becomes labelled 'creative'. For Kuhn (1970), the accidental, premeditated or cumulative fracturing of existing paradigms is the only way that science truly advances.

Creative Analysis of Observational Data

Strauss and Corbin (1991) allow creativity into a very orderly scheme of analysis by suggesting that manipulation of categorized data is, itself, a creative enterprise. However, this seems a distant relation of more popular understanding of the term, creativity. Their view conflates creativity with 'theoretical sensitivity':

> Theoretical sensitivity represents an important creative aspect of grounded theory. This sensitivity represents an ability not only to use personal and professional experience imaginatively, but also literature. It enables the analyst to see the research situation and its associated data in new ways, and to explore the data's potential for developing theory.

They walk the careful line between wanting their approach viewed as science whilst accepting that creativity is, nevertheless, a formative ingredient. They deal with the latter by application of formal procedures, to ensure that the creative elements are systematized. There are computer programs now which can sweep through qualitative data and help the researcher pattern and cluster words and phrases. Are they, therefore, in Strauss and Corbin's terms, creative?

Giddens (1991) more typically, pays faint scientistic compliments to Strauss and Corbin's creative imagination, by demoting it to a skill in sociological research:

> A large part of the skill of identifying worthwhile sociological research consists of correctly identifying puzzles.

Again, the theme of undue respect for scientific convention is apparent. It is mainly in very general philosophic statements that writers on methodology accept a fuller view of creativity in the analytic process:

> Imagination is our means of interpreting the world. (Warnock, 1970)

A strong critique of the orthodox delimiting of creativity in qualitative (and other) research would suggest that its rewriting as puzzle solving or mechanistic ordering, is the result of a regulatory power principle which seeks to justify research institutions' hegemony within society. Accepting the essential anarchic presence of creativity within research, liberates discourse in unpredictable ways.

Bohm and Pleat (1988) explore this issue by looking, as Kuhn did, at how new knowledge comes into being. They draw a distinction between the reordering of knowledge, 'endarkenment' and insightful change 'enlightenment'. The reordering of knowledge remains part of the hidden conservatism of research discourse whilst insightful processes remove blocks and fixed conceptions about the world we inhabit. The former is a passive, abstract knowledge waiting to be used and reordered in our data stores whilst the latter is active and, similar to Polanyi's (1969) notion of tacit knowledge, is an uncontrolled but vital part of us which can be let loose in our interpretations of the world. Famous examples abound regarding the way in which imagination has pointed the direction of new knowledge; Newton's prefiguring of gravity, Einstein's of relativity, Kekule's vision of the snake eating its own tail giving him the key to the benzine ring. The visionary experience in all cases was prefaced by intense periods of concentrated work. The vision paved the way for a third phase, that of developing the insight as a hypothesis which could be developed into formal, logical structures of knowledge. Without these imaginative leaps, formal structures continually lead us back into what we know already.

The difficulty for qualitative research is that unlike the work of the eminent figures cited above, the researcher is not trying to solve highly focused problems. Rather, the field tends to be a diffuse, implicated set of interrelated issues which include the researcher, the impact of the research and a process of continual contemporaneous change. Whilst imaginative responses to problems abound at every level and phase of research, they never appear as significant as the above examples from the history of scientific ideas. However, drawing together personal experience, the literature of the imagination and some trawling of the research literature, what follows are seven ways in which mundane research might be able to transcend its role as a conservative mirror of the field of study. They may represent a way towards paradigmatic erosions and shifts which are vital to the critical movement of thought and action in both the research community and for the person on the street. Needless to say, what follows can be used as much to obfuscate critical thought as to illuminate it!

Seven Types of Creativity in Data Analysis

Seven types of creativity are included here. They are not the complete set, obviously, nor are they mutually exclusive but it was with Empson's book as a starting point, quoted at the beginning of this chapter, that I was led into its writing. Rather than see them as separate approaches or strategies, it is better to accept them as having some distinct characteristics and some degree of overlap.

1 Labels and Categories

The commonest technique in drawing attention to a problem, be it old or new, is by introducing a label which contains novel metaphoric characteristics. Thus, terms such as *juvenile delinquency, maladjustment, progressive schooling, student-centredness, sink and magnet schools, democratic evaluation, action research, thick description, a snapshot in time, illuminative evaluation, paradigm,* may precipitate and enrich initial debate. But only initially. Labelling and categorizing is an intensely competitive business. Without substance to underpin new language, it can lead quickly to endarkenment. The hit parade of 'in' terms changes rapidly.

In an attempt to offset researcher domination of the 'naming of parts', John Schostak and I (Sanger, 1989b) appropriated the labels and categories that teachers invented or commonly utilized in their discourse, to guide us in finding significance in data. Terms such as *disconnected question, negotiation or social chat*, produced vital new directions for the action research team, a power-sharing over language and new ways of constructing consequent explanations of classroom experience. All the terms were coined to explain the events that teachers began to observe afresh, when they became involved in action research.

Disconnected questions, for example, led us to follow up any questions from students which seemed unrelated to the content focus of teaching and learning. Teachers tended previously to discount, evade, ignore or not hear such questions. However, once heard on cassette recorders or seen on video, they became hard to ignore. By following them up, the researching group were afforded entry into students' learning strategies, learning hierarchies and agendas of concern from which they had previously been excluded.

2 Methodological Imports

The introduction of methodological approaches from other fields is a common procedure in energizing the research process. Whether such imports are being used as explanatory metaphors or as strategic models, the effect on the way we see data can be, at the least, cathartic. Thus, educational research and evaluation discovers literary criticism, connoisseurship, therapy, action research, a range of sociological variations, fiction, biography, feminist distrust, reception theory and so on.

Two examples that have affected my own practice are homoeopathy (see chapter 11) and Roland Barthes' musings on photography (see chapter 3). Studying the way that homoeopathy is said to effect cures, in contradiction to mainstream or allopathic medicine, provided an insight into a way of conducting classroom, ward or canteen evaluation. Essentially the homoeopathic practitioner attempts to treat the whole person by providing a poison which elicits the total range of symptoms that the patient is presenting — albeit in extraordinarily insignificant dosages. These tiny doses can be 'read' by the body, which raises its armies of immunity to the poison — and thus to the prevailing illness, *which had, hitherto, completely besieged the body's power to diagnose what was wrong*. Utilising this model in social settings led me to re-present small, representative examples of the worst excesses, problems, concerns, interactions, decisions to individuals and groups, for their reflection. Wholesale re-presentation of data could lead to a spiral into further trouble. The art became to find the right dose, the perfect selection from the data. For individual teachers it might be the description of a speech pattern, repeated observations of some element of body language, an aspect of classroom management; for organizations it might be the setting for meetings, signage in the corridors, the architecture of sin bins. Utilizing the homoeopathic model has helped me ration and refine evaluative feedback — in other words, analyze what might be therapeutic in the data.

Roland Barthes in *Camera Lucida* (1982), utilizes a similar technique but for personal, therapeutic, illuminative purposes. By searching photographs for two methodological elements, which he calls the punctum and the studium, he raises his critical interest in those photographs which have explanatory or generative power. The studium is the term he uses for the field to which the photograph belongs, for example, family portraits, nudes, war, landscapes. The punctum is that, usually singular, item within the photograph which creates a focus of disturbance in the observer. It might be a shirt, a belt, the sheet being carried to cover a body in a street or the way a hand is flexed. For me, it has raised awareness of which data I might be drawn to in my own studium (the classroom, the canteen, the playground, the shop floor); and the elements within each studium which arrest my attention, cause a frisson — and why. Thus it is, that data become signified at the outset which have an explanatory power through their capacity to disrupt the field of understanding — or that are discovered later to have the Barthes' gift of generating insight (a notice board, the placing of the teacher's desk, the organization of the reception area in a school, the way hands are raised in a particular classroom). It leads us back into the familiar, with the presence of mind to try to review it as possibly exotic.

3   Theoretical Imports

Being challenged critically by theories and philosophies has its effect upon the way we see the world. Even in the act of repudiating theory, we are forced to articulate more clearly what it is that we do hold dear. Reading beyond the substantive focus of research can stretch our models of inquiry, even to breaking point. Naturalistic enquiry, for example, for those who trace the lineage to Gadamer (1975), may be seen through the light of cultural materialism as evidencing a cosy meritocratic glow of liberal humanism, at once patronising, club-like and conservative. For those obsessed with the current cult of autobiography as a research method, a decent leavening of Derrida's literary theory (1978) would make them examine assumptions about personal histories, whose they are and what data they actually provide the research community. The conception that a history can be **personal** is held up to question. Its institutionalization as an aspect of academic endeavour severs further its credibility in offering a way towards tacit understandings. Husserlian bracketing (1964), Habermas's (1971) critical discourse or Garfinkel's (1967) ethnomethodology may each be introduced to destabilize our preconceptions in ways similar to approaches the Russian Formalists explored in literary criticism. In order to write this chapter, which can be seen as an autobiographical text, carefully selected incidents and carefully chosen literature, combine to construct an event for an audience. Premeditation has already given way to the 'excess' which Derrida avers will always seep out of my attempt to tie language down. Intensive reading across a wide range of literature undoubtedly leads the writer to just such excess. And in it the researcher may find novel insights and unusual workings of the imagination.

And even though Strauss and Corbin (1991) prove, at the end of the day, too mechanistic in their methodology for this author, their data manipulation may well be the external force other researchers need, to gain new handles on their research enterprise.

4 Novel Methods

A way of guarding against endarkenment is by the invention of data gathering methods to suit the circumstances. Just because they don't appear in text books and haven't been evaluated for their potential robustness, doesn't mean they cannot provide insights that defy the sweep of formal methods. Too often, researchers remain faithfully within their methodiocal mind set and (for example) merely interview, observe and analyze documentation. Data, however, may be generated via more interventive researcher actions, without necessarily influencing the complexion of the findings. Since teaching and learning is the subject of much of my work, I turn to teachers and learners often to aid me with methodology. Here are some examples:

- asking children to mark pieces of work as though they were the teacher and recording their logics in doing it (researching learning within the marking process);
- asking pupils what their mark is going to be and what comments they expect to find on their work, before their books are handed back (researching learning within the marking process);
- use of drawings, cartoons, metaphors, colour spectrum (see *6 below*);
- having teachers and students discuss their class by analysing a video-tape of it (similarly with groups of teachers and curriculum meetings, interviews for new posts etc);
- new kinds of check lists as, for example, this one a teacher produced, to use while she walked round her class (see page 56):

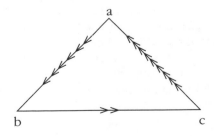

- feeding back observations as stories — having respondents edit them;
- creating critical incidents in case study form, to discover cultural responses to moral issues.

What is at issue is the means by which the researcher can transform etic inquiry into emic. The researcher may often need to produce some destabilization in the normal flow of the research field, in order to enable participants to reflect critically upon what they regard as 'normal', habitual or ritualistic. Seeing yourself as others see you, can often be the basis of this. Thus a liberal progressive teacher, believing in student-centredness, sees herself taking students' work from them as they sit in their desks. She looks through it, makes a mark or two on it and hands it back. She is shocked. The whole body language represents power and control.

5 Reporting

There is a cliche in research, which roughly goes, 'writing yourself into knowledge'. It is based on what has been stated above. The act of writing is an act of analysis. The ordering, weighing, listing, juxtaposing and bridging of information, changes the nature of that information. If the writer falls into metaphor, then the process is exacerbated. Attempts to clarify what the researcher thinks s/he knows results in discoveries of nuances which had lain dormant, hitherto. Most researchers write throughout the various phases of research. They make plans, called designs, they make descriptive notes, they transcribe, they analyze and they report. At any of these stages, a deliberate alteration in 'the moving finger', writing, can begin a process which leads to different and sometimes new conceptions. For example, if the researcher determines to complete every sentence during observation, rather than make shorthand accounts, the data is less malleable at a later stage because sentences and paragraphs are less tractable and often have a holistic unity from which it is difficult to disengage. What happens to all those observational recordings? They don't appear in reports in their integrity. They often become an influence, a background and occasionally a highlight to emphasize some analytical point. Few reports allow the observations to stand in their entirety so that the reader can judge actions or make interpretations. In a report to the British Film Institute (Sanger, 1993), I presented a selection of raw data at the beginning of the report. The reader was asked to develop opinions about what underlay individuals' behaviour, as documented. Then they could be freer to mount a critique of my own interpretations and analyses.

Interpretations of data at each of these stages may be closed or open. Do we, self or unconsciously leave enough open to ease the clear-up at the end? The tying of knots? If we believe the world contains contingent rather than casual events, why do we look for overall coherence? Why are our research reports so logically ordered? So causally driven?

6 Metaphors

Look at the metaphors in the data and you begin to comprehend the internal critical tensions of the population under scrutiny. It is a form of content analysis. In an excellent feminist critique of Peter Berger's much used text book, *An Invitation to Sociology*, Reinhartz (1988) literally unhinges any notion that Berger is free from some deep-seated chauvinist attitudes to half the population he studies. This reputable and highly influential writer calls women 'station wagons', says that sociologists as small boys may have become sociologists after peering through keyholes at maiden aunts undressing and compares heroic bomber crews to mindless women shoppers in supermarkets.

In an analysis of the conversational data in a classroom of gifted children in Canada (see Chapter 8), I turned from my usual pursuit of observing and recording verbal and non-verbal processes and began, instead, examining the metaphoric content of pupils' talk by playing and replaying a video recording. Suddenly, there appeared before me (and a group of teachers I was leading in the analysis) a torrent of strange, dark images of death and disease. My synopsis of this torrent was as follows:

> So I looked at the content. The poetic image of a sick fly with its many literary and film connotations from Blake to Goldblum, caught my immediate attention. I began to note the words and images which seemed linked to the metaphor of the sick fly.

> > fly, sick, die, unnatural causes, old age, sickness, disease, heart attack, shot, Aunt and Dad dropped dead, virus, bacteria, foreign, injury, afflicted, germ warfare, skin, infection, ill, vomiting, nauseous, disgusting, insane, heart disease, alien, fester, blood, germs, carriers, haemophiliacs, hospital, stick a knife into Marie . . .

The point needs to be made that neither the teachers analyzing the videotape of the class, nor I, were aware of this level of language use on a first viewing. The data were suddenly perplexing. There was a sense in which the language content was providing an eerie critique of selective schooling for gifted children. To be gifted in that class may not have led to the quality experience some would have wished when providing for their special education (Sanger, 1989a). Yet other ways of interpreting the classroom had not suggested any threat to a vision of a group of motivated and stable pupils. The class was student-centred, pupils grasped the agenda, obeyed rules of philosophic discourse, listened carefully to each other and treated the teacher as a resource.

I have worked for a decade with a group of headteachers who have asked staff to describe their work in drawings, verses or other word images. These seem to provide more poignancy than conversation normally produces and offer an immediate starting point for in-depth discussion of the way that the personal informs the professional (Sanger, 1992).

7 Alien Structures

There is a pile of data in front of me. I can set about the sometime endarkening process of looking for patterns and developing by induction, reasons why individuals and groups seem to be doing this or that. But supposing I adopt some external structure in which to fit the data? What happens? The data begin to lose their familiarity. And even their mundaneness. These structures may be the classifications used in the field by participants (see 1 above), ways of seeing adopted by other fields of enquiry or simply frameworks that make the researcher think in new ways.

When I adopted an A–Z of issues in information handling (Sanger, 1989b), in order to give analysis more accessibility, I was presented with a puzzle over several of the letters in the alphabet. X for example. The word which I elicited from the dictionary was xenogenesis — the capacity of the parent to produce offspring unlike itself. Just so with teachers — the capacity to produce learners unlike themselves, an absolutely essential ingredient in student-centred learning. It was a key concept, but one which arrived at the analytical level because of the structuring of the issues emanating from the action research data. The whole A–Z with its twenty-six categories of issue, made me think comprehensively about the data, logically, in terms of whether each was a separate category or a sub-set of another and creatively, in terms of what might be there in the data for which I had not accounted.

Within the same action research project, a teacher analyzed his mathematics classroom interactions in terms of primary colours and mixes to produce further tones (Whittaker, 1989). Warnock (1970) says that our imagination may, 'render our experience unfamiliar and mysterious'. Thus it becomes data rich and capable of producing new insights.

Postscript

What has been described above is a practical beginning to the debate about how we might utilize creativity in data analysis. Much more needs to be done in analyzing how we come up with novel ideas, strategies and hypotheses. Koestler (1989) sees structural resemblances to the QED in mathematics and the punch-line of a joke. Essentially it concerns putting knowns together and coming up with a striking unknown which makes new sense of what precedes it. Much of what has been covered above contains Koestler's structure. Research would, no doubt, be much better for the discovery that its processes structurally resemble good jokes. As in this French irregular verb.

Je Lacan

Tu ne comprend pas

10   Closely Observed Training

I was commissioned through a Home Office Project to generate a series of case studies for police training. On one occasion I was involved in their handling of football crowds. On a Saturday morning before a match involving Norwich City and Tottenham Hotspur, I joined all the police involved in a meal in a local school. It was euphemistically called 'operational feeding'. Everyone was there when I arrived with a very senior officer. I was wearing jeans and a leather jacket, ready to inveigle myself into the very heart of the Barclay stand, where the rowdiest supporters would be. As we walked through the serried ranks, deep into their main course, I caught many covert stares and whispers. And a sort of peculiar respect. 'Such is the power of research in the police force', I thought. The senior officer spoke, as we sat down. 'They think you're Special Branch'. 'I forgot to tell them you'd be here.' He smiled and patted the bulge of the cassette recorder in my jacket pocket. 'Gun?'

The public sector climate in the late twentieth century is a confused melange of innovation, change, conflict between centrism and localism and issues of public accountability, assessment and organizational evaluation. At whatever level and in whatever role, individuals are being required to analyze and make transparent their practice. We are in an age of rationalism where economic criteria dominate educational ideals, where training philosophy and the managerial imperative would exert greater influence by the day upon the complex life of the workplace. Where every human act is reduced to competency and skill.

However, fortunately, it is the complexity of social life which defeats this charge of technocracy. The vast majority of teachers know that classrooms are both unpredictable and idiosyncratic, police know that human acts and evidence of these acts are riddled with ambiguity and nurses know that patients are unique and their recovery time completely unpredictable. They all know that as participant observers of their own practices, they realize the complexity better than any outsider — and even then they may be aware of how slim this understanding is. Teachers who begin to research and reflect upon their classroom experience constantly expose the deficiencies in their conceptualizations of the relationship between learning and their teaching approaches.

No matter how sophisticated the instrumentation of appraisal schemes, the checklists, the schedules, the structured interviews, nor how experienced the classroom observer, the central problem remains unresolved. What is actually happening in classrooms? How do we determine its value? There is enough evidence since the curriculum reform movement of the 1960s onwards to show that the claims for reform always prove exaggerated once consequences in classrooms are investigated. That causality gives way to weak forms of contingency.

The rhetoric/reality divide has always been evident in discourses of social action. Every practitioner has theories about what is or what is not successful in the workplace. The theories may be more implicit than explicit but they add up to a general set of attitudes which, in the normal run of things, is not tested within, or by, practitioners. What it does lead to is an unsubstantiated judgmentalism in relation to practice issues and concerns. And it appears to be so at all levels. Institutional rhetoric becomes justified by expositions of policy implementation in weighty documents. It is only when evaluation begins to examine where rhetoric meets reality, whether in management, administration or practice, that the gap can be seen for what it is. Therein lies the basis for unlimited conflict as individuals and groups fight to maintain their rhetoric and insist that their practice substantiates it. In such circumstances it is often the evaluative process which is attacked by all sides as a result of having exposed dissonances within the system.

What has this to do with workshops on classroom observation? It seems right to point out a little of the context in which such workshops are being run. The administration wants clearer understandings of how policy is implemented in the classroom, either to modify policy or to change practitioners' attitudes and strategies through in-service courses. Practitioners, for their part, may grudgingly accept that their work requires some form of scrutiny, or change will never really occur. However, they distrust being observed because they know full well that such observations could lead to forms of assessment which could damage their professional careers. Much of the 'new money' in the public sector over the last twenty years is tied to evaluation and assessment in some guise. Accountability made public. Such evaluation often seeks to look at those areas of practice where the application of national or local policy comes to fruition or disarray.

Whether observation workshops are part of training towards practitioner appraisal or are part of a policy on staff development, curriculum development or institutional self-evaluation, the central dilemma for the sponsors of the workshops concerns the effects such observations might have on institutional life and the relationship between institutions and central policy. Should observations become linked with surveillance in practitioners' minds, then conflict will ensue. Should observations be too bland then no effects are likely to be seen. Should observations be too technical then practitioners will reject their mystification and instrumentalism. And so the dilemma intensifies. The experience of this author, whether in England or abroad, is that practitioners are ill-equipped *because of their traditional roles in organizations and a consequent tendency to operate from untested generalizations about their working practices* to effect observations which enhance the potential of colleagues to reflect and change. They often have neither a developed sense of principles nor an established set of procedures from which to undertake observational support within their institutions. And yet, much of in-service support points not at institutional infrastructure and the delicacy of human relations but towards tooling up practitioners in technical methodologies. Essentially, workplace observation tends to be taught as though it is a free-standing module within a research repertoire. The likely consequence is that participants in training suffer an exacerbation of the technocratic tendencies of institutional management to the detriment of both institutional warmth and collegiality. They may also alienate their fellow practitioners from a corporate search for better understanding and sharing of practice.

This chapter sets out to summarize the structures and strategies which have been effective in the observation workshops this author has run, why they have been effective and what the consequences have been for professional practice.

Conceptual Framework for Observation Workshops

Observation is a practical activity guided by a rationale related to some form of purpose. We observe for a reason. The reason leads us to formulate what we will look at and how we will look at it. We have to organize our workshop activities so that participants can experience doing observation and disentangling the act of observation from the political, social and practical context which requires them to make observations.

Making observations has far-reaching consequences for both observers and the observed. In order to limit damage in observational practice we must ensure that participants move safely from the simulated to the real. Workshops should end with workplace observations and not start with them.

In order to ensure that the damage that can be done through acts of observation is minimal when they leave a workshop, we must be certain that participants understand and can construct a contract of principles of procedures *which are basic to any act of observation.*

Practitioners tend to imagine that observation is merely a matter of looking and telling. Would that it were so. Observers need to experience and articulate the difficulties of trying to do observations without tacit or explicit prejudice and preformed conceptual categories. They need to be challenged at deep levels by facilitator or group critique, and issues addressed which may be uncomfortable; issues such as motivation, ideology or gender.

There are many myths concerning observation. The major one is that scientific respectability demands that practitioner observations should be unambiguous, objective, rigorous and thus be amenable to being translated into numbers for detached, computer-based, clinical analysis. A workshop should

provide practitioners with time to try out the full range of observational strategies and instruments so that they understand the shortcomings of each, realise the place of the observer in meaning-making and the extraordinary range
of influences on the observational process. Participants should have experience in handling issues of subjectivity and objectivity, judgmentalism, power,
politics, ambiguity and so on.

Central to the learning philosophy of such workshops, is the pedagogical
expedient of challenging participants' deeply held convictions. This is done by
gathering evidence against the gut rhetoric of speculation. Ask participants
what they have seen in a video. Ask them then to provide a hypothesis concerning what they have just seen, such *as the child is uncommunicative* or *the
teacher spends too much time at her desk* or *the teacher is insensitive to individual needs.* Ask them to test this hypothesis by gathering evidence. Invariably,
intense self-evaluation occurs as disparities emerge between what they felt
sure was there and what was actually there, on the videotape.

There is a natural cycle to workplace observation: negotiating access;
negotiating focus; negotiating the method of observation; observing; negotiating further meetings and dialogue related to the observation; negotiating the
observer's rights to hold a copy or to use the observationa data in different
contexts.

Workshops should be highly interactive, with plenty of opportunity for
less formal, small group activity so that participants have a full opportunity to
reflect and articulate their more private opinions and feelings.

Workshops should have a cumulative brief so that participants sense a
learning direction in their activities and can see the practical benefits of their
learning to their professional practice. The workshop might be designed for
classroom, ward, beat, or field social work, as part of a larger brief, such as the
introduction of appraisal, improvement in professional practice, the development of a research perspective in professional work or the drawing up of
ethical procedures for research in the workplace. Workshop organizers should
develop a style of working with groups which is consonant with their aims for
the workshop and the eventual applications in the workplace. In the model
suggested here, the organizer should withdraw as much as possible to a responsive role, feeding in alternative analyses to broaden understanding, offering intercessions when groups need advice from experienced practitioners and
concentrating upon the contextual implications of the workshop for each group
member.

An Example of Training for Observation

The following timetable was negotiated with the Nottinghamshire Inspectorate
for an in-service course for Curriculum and Staff Development Coordinators in
September 1986. It is a four-day residential workshop. There are twenty-nine
teachers from primary, secondary and further education institutions.

DAY ONE

9.30–10.30 Introduction and Overview
A general introduction to the course. Some biography of Jack Sanger to
reduce teacher group resistance to an outsider and an 'academic' emphasizing his long teaching biography and ensure credibility. Overview of the
week. The purpose of this session is to set the tone for the four days,
particularly emphasizing the practical, educational and political principles
which had been brought to bear on its organization. The group are encouraged to feel that it was their course and their agenda would prevail.
The cumulative task was mentioned.

10.45–12.30 Simulation Exercise
An exercise where five sub-groups choose a teacher and observers. The
teacher is sent off for half-an-hour to prepare a lesson of his/her choice.
The groups are given an observational task in relation to the proposed
lesson. Each group has a different task. The tasks involve:

- making a specific checklist to cover one aspect of teaching, to be
  used by the whole group as an introduction to triangulation;
- discussing 'good teaching' and entering the observational phase
  with a blank sheet, with ensuing triangulation;
- dividing up the teaching process into broad areas for which
  each group member can take responsibility. Subsequently they
  can create a comprehensive record;
- portraying the lesson via individual narratives and as comprehensively as possible, again for triangulation;
- one group negotiating with the teacher the focus and methods of
  observation to be used.

The teachers teach for fifteen minutes while their respective groups make
their observations. The groups then report back to their teachers and, with
them, prepare presentations of the experience for a plenary session in the
afternoon. At this session they are to present the pitfalls, problematics and
benefits of the chosen 'style' of observation and interaction each has used.

1.45–3.15 Simulation Debriefing in Plenary
The five groups provide ten minute feedback presentations with a ten
minute follow-up for critical debate amongst the whole group. A workshop starting this way enables participation, drama and the beginning of
a focus on the issues without subjecting any individual or group to too
much threat to established values or professional esteem. By not reporting
on substantive issues of teacher activity but focusing upon the issues
within the observational process, they begin to realise the complexity of
their future role in an institution.

3.30–6.15 Principles and Procedures

In this session the sub-groups draw up a draft of the principles and procedures which are required to guarantee ethical propriety in institutional work between colleagues. Reflecting on their experience of the day in this case may bring out, for example, that tight negotiation is essential between observer and teacher, that data generated in the classroom should be 'owned' by the teacher and that the observer should not undertake instrumentation which is unwieldy or mystifying or too complex to be of immediate use. The following illustration is an example of the kind of lists that are drawn up. All lists are photocopied and distributed between groups for maximum learning.

Principles and procedures

- To inform classroom practice
- To support the teacher
- To raise the general awareness of educational practice
- To realize that observation is a limited instrument
- To negotiate at all stages
- To maintain confidentiality and professionalism
- To provide a basis for feedback and discussion.

Observation should be by invitation only. Agree timing of:
(a) Initial discussion: discuss principles and negotiate contract
(b) Observation — followed by reflection time
(c) Feedback: write up a short report, feed it back within twenty-four hours

---

This is the beginning of a cumulative task for this workshop. The idea is that individuals, over the course of four days, will gradually refine the list of principles and procedures, as a result of their experience, which will serve them well when they return to schools. It provides the double function of underlining how important are the ethical considerations in undertaking this kind of activity in schools or colleges and providing a basis for institutional policy in the use of observation.

7.30–9.00 Observational Literature

There should be a range of observational literature provided for the groups to browse through, criticise in small groups and, generally, expand their theoretical understanding of the activity. (In the normal run of things, practitioners don't have the opportunity to read, or they find research and allied literature too distant or coded, to maintain interest. Given the immediacy of experience and the availability of the literature, many read research papers for the first time for years, at these workshops.

DAY TWO

9.00–10.00 Principles and Procedures
The workshop leader runs an analytical discussion which compares and contrasts the small group lists of principles and procedures developed the previous evening. Again the focus is on ethics before action. The teachers become more critical as they can see the contrasts in the working documents they have prepared.

10.30–12.30 Video-Observation
The group in its sub-groups all watch a half-hour research video of a working classroom. By research video is meant a mostly panoramic view of activity, without directorial influences creating close ups and slow pans. They then disperse to prepare, in sub-groups, an observational schedule or process to review the same half hour's viewing. They can concentrate on any aspect of the lesson.

1.45–3.45 Review Video and Prepare Presentations
The video is shown again and the groups use their schedules. They spend time in their groups analyzing the results of their work and preparing an OHP presentation on the efficacy or otherwise of their observational approach.

4.00–6.15 OHP Presentations
This period consists of fifteen-minute presentations and ten-minute whole group responsive discussions. Issues are collected on a flip chart as they arise. This simulation represents a step forward from the last. The emphasis is more firmly on observational methods, the classroom is real, if on video, and the groups have the opportunity to match their instrumentation to particular events with which they have been familiarized. Dissonances between first and second viewing, the partiality of observational methods and the difficulties in maintaining focus and rigour are highlighted by the experience. It is at about this point that participants really grasp the true nature of bias and judgment, positive and negative critique and the complexity of the task of providing an adequate and stimulating observational service to fellow practitioners.

7.30–9.00 Update Principles and Procedures
The group return to their original lists and modify them in the light of the day's experiences. Further research video material is provided for browsing and practising observation.

DAY THREE

9.00–10.00 Principles and Procedures
The revised lists of principles and procedures are compared and contrasted, analyzed and criticized as to their utility, ethics and practicability.

10.30–11.30 Escher Slides

A dozen or so slides of the work of Maurice Escher are used as the basis for discussion about perception, bias, biography and understanding. The slides seem to provide an important turning point in a week's workshop. By working through analogy, displacement and the abstract, groups feel freer to extrapolate from the images in front of them to the more concrete world of the classroom. Some regard the experience in an almost mystical light. Because Escher's work defies logic and creates enormous dissonance within perception, it is as though practitioners reach deep within themselves to give their professional selves a greater personal texture.

11.30–12.30 Homeopathy and Hot Storage

At this point ways of operating as an observer are presented to the group which explore a rationalization of practice in school or college contexts; what can be done, how it can be done and in what circumstances so that problems of local politics: hierarchy, assessment and autonomy. Are alleviated. This session provides an acceleration to the upswing of the four days. After experiencing the various ways that observations can be constructed and undertaken, the problems and pitfalls, teachers reach a low ebb of enthusiasm as they consider how difficult it is to be both meaningful and non-judgmental in their service to their fellows. This session tries to open a way to parsimonious support which also stimulates reflection and change. For full treatment of these issues, see Sanger (1986). Reference is made to the homeopathy of observational report in chapter 8.

1.45–3.45 Video Observation

An imaginary brief is given to the group by myself, representing the teacher in the next video. This is to be a lesson in which they each must negotiate an observation. They work as individuals and prepare an observation schedule before viewing and applying it to the half-hour video of classroom life. Afterwards they must show their raw data, together with a short report, summing up their findings, to me, as the teacher.

4.00–6.15 Report Critique

Reports are criticized in sub-groups. Then the groups feed back in plenary some of the issues that have arisen in those discussions. Again, the emphasis is upon process. The agenda is expanded, now, to include reporting as a feature of observational support. The simulation pushes the group further towards real time observation. With no chance to review the video they have deadlines to meet. Being very well versed by now in the processes of observation and with growing certainties of principle and procedure, their criticism of their reporting is much more acute.

7.30–9.00 Update Principles and Procedures

A continuation of the cumulative task of the workshop. Research videos for practice.

DAY FOUR

9.00–12.30 School and College Observations
All the group go out to their own schools and colleges, negotiating and doing observations, generating reports and feeding back to their teachers. The morning in institutions is set up earlier in the week. The group know that they are working towards this event. By this time they are well prepared for the process but are healthily anxious about presenting themselves and their role in an acceptable light to their colleagues.

1.45–4.00 Debriefing
Working first in sub-groups and then in plenary, the processes of the morning are analyzed and conclusions drawn about the move to real institutional work.

4.30–6.00 Final Working Draft of Principles and Procedures
As individuals the group draws up their working list of principles and procedures for return to their places of work. These will be circulated to all staff and a final, agreed, institutional set of guidelines, produced.

As can be seen from the example quoted above, the intent of the organizer is gradually to intensify the focus on observation by employing an experiential learning base, by continual return to principles and procedures and by judicious inputs from the organizer where appropriate. The aim is to ensure that what is learned has been internalized and that each member of the group will adopt a responsive and responsible role in their dealings with fellow staff.

Several concepts are woven into the discourse, through the week, by the organizer. The first is that by recognizing the limitations of observation, we can proceed to what is practically possible. The role relationship between observer and observed is critical. The observer must enable the observed to take charge of the process and use the observer as a service agency for support in whatever mode the observed practitioner deems useful. There are ways of creating greater parity in that role relationship. There are techniques for improving the quality of observation and the neutrality of that observation. There are procedures which limit the effect the observer has upon the class. We must start where the teacher is at the point of entry into the classroom. His/her biography, teaching style and classroom management must be respected at the outset. No attempt must be made to impose external theories of change, ideologies or offer advice. Instead, the teacher is encouraged to own, view, and analyze observational data and take appropriate steps according to his/her perception of the data. A primary objective of classroom observation is to leave the teacher at the end of the process more willing to have observers present, more willing to talk about educational processes and more likely to question what he/she is doing in the classroom with the possibility of innovating as a consequence.

If observational workshops are based on traditional research approaches they fail to take account of institutional context, individual biography and what is possible with any particular individual or in any particular institution. The assumption behind a workshop such as this is that if schools, hospital wards, police canteens or managerial activities are going to change and respond to new initiatives, then staff need to become more reflective with regard to their practice, more open in that practice and more involved in the educational discourse of their institutions and the larger systems in which they operate. Workshops, therefore, require constant reference to practical contexts, which include the levels of capability of staff when they become observers as opposed to their expertise as main grade teachers, heads of department or heads of school. Observational work may be initiated by experienced individuals at the outset but if observations are to become a whole institution enterprise then practising teachers will have to engage in the process. How they are inducted into that process by their more experienced colleagues will depend on how well those colleagues learned their lessons on INSET workshops.

11 Administering Poison: Reporting Observations

> Auden once suggested that a literary critic should declare his 'dream of Eden' because 'honesty demands that he describe it to his readers, so that they may be in a position to judge his judgments'. (Phillips, 1994)

Having our readers respond favourably to our descriptions of them and their activities, is, of course, a key issue to research and evaluation. I am not using the term 'favourably' in the sense that they should be pleased about it, necessarily, but rather that they should be favourably disposed to the intent and its execution. That they learn to trust our professionalism. Perhaps that they should feel the researcher is behaving within an agreed remit, that the feedback is fair and accurate and that bias or prejudice are not acting as unseen contaminating filters within the process of reconstruction. All this seems desirable. It is a step forward from the days when we would hide behind a smoke screen of anonymity, authorial neutrality and scientific objectivity.

In our recognition of plural perspectives and contextual ambiguity, we need to convince our audiences that we are coming as clean as we can, when we depict social events. That we draw out the biases in ourselves as observers. Then our respondents can review our words and seek new readings of our constructs. This would seem to be the answer to the post-modern nightmare of plural readings, endless chains of signification, reception theory and the like. But it is hard to accomplish. Taking Auden's line at the beginning of this chapter as a guide, can you imagine the response to the researcher when she announces that she believes in intensive farming and then goes on to expect to conduct penetrative interviews with her population of animal rights activists, or negotiate a vantage point to observe their acts of public disorder? In some respects, respondents want to believe in our neutrality. They want to believe in our unimpeachable evidence and, as often as not, in our intelligent interpretations. They don't want to have the responsibility of unmasking us and finding the same old next door humanity under our professional garb. Thus it is that researchers end up making themselves responsible for their respondents. We develop ethical protocols to limit our capacity to do harm. We use the language of self-denigration in that we are parsimonious in our claims for validity or comprehensiveness.

Thinking through this issue, it seemed to me that we can, at least, reduce the threat of grand narratives and greater truths subordinating our readership's capacity to be critical of our methods and outcomes. If 'coming out' with what we believe, is a problem, and if our portrayals of people and events carry within them the seeds of imperialism because of our attempts to cover all ambiguities, perspectives and lines of reasonable interpretation, then we should adopt a method of reporting which gives more power to the reader to be critical, thoughtful and, even, act upon our material.

There is plenty of evidence to support the contention that research and evaluation of professional practices generally lack impact, particularly in terms of meaningful individual and institutional change. Rather than developing insights which enable decisions to be made and actions to be undertaken, the accumulated insights of research and evaluation activity lose their valuable glint in the offertory box of written reports. Utilization of reporting may be affected by a number of interrelated factors. Barbara Dickey (1980) constructed something like the following list:

- degree of involvement and attitudes of decision-makers to the research/evaluation as a whole;
- the evident quality of the research (an arbitrary factor in some evaluators' experiences!);
- the degree of recommendation (the more far-reaching, the less likely to be implemented!);
- whether the research/evaluation has a formative or summative approach (the former, being more integrated with practice, tends to have greater utility);
- timeliness;
- complexity of language;
- length;
- format.

Of course these are only some of the factors which comprise the possible utilization of research and evaluation reporting: See MacDonald (1980) and Simons (1980) for more detailed and complex scenarios. When we focus on observation activity, as a prime strategy for information gathering and exchange within research and evaluation, all that Dickey suggests is extremely pertinent. It is a complicated task to inform, with or without prescription, in the lived-in and never static world of social action. What follows offers the rudiments of an action approach to the communication problem which researchers and evaluators might bear in mind when they begin their next round of negotiating their viewpoints with participants. It is envisaged that the adoption of this alternative approach may provide the evaluator with an effective, naturalistic method for increasing the utilization of his/her reporting.

It needed two conditions, then, to turn a stick into a hobby horse: first, that its form made it just possible to ride on it; secondly — and

perhaps decisively — that riding mattered. (E.H. Gombrich, *Medita
tions on a Hobby Horse*)

Research and evaluation reporting may need, as with Gombrich's hobby horse,
two conditions to turn them from a mass of inert data into vehicles of action.
The first condition is that reporting is assimilable and the second that its users
feel it to be relevant: that is, that it represents a focussing of attention, a
reflection on events which may illuminate current complexity or inform further
action. It is difficult to escape nagging worries concerning the process of
reporting; the attempted portrayals of people, objects and events; the analyses,
the judgments. In naturalistic enquiry there always remains the technical and/
or artistic problems of representing the 'field' in such a way as to provide
persuasive evidence of its complex pathology whilst achieving enough verisi-
militude for the participants to recognize their context, assimilate others' experiences and to have consciousness raised to enable them to explore a range
of interpretations beyond those included within the report. To move beyond
the information given

There are two approaches to the representation of individuals and organizations via observation, depending on the aforesaid summative or formative
aspirations of the researcher. In one, observations attempt to describe what is
inside the hermeneutic circle (Gauld and Shotter, 1977), or the case study
parameters which define the constituency or bounded system of the project,
programme or working area, to those outside. In the other, they hope to raise
the consciousness of *both* those within and without that same circle, with
regard to the issues, events and contexts of the study. This dual aspiration may
not be part of all evaluators' agendas but has certainly become part of the
rhetoric of various authorities in the field of qualitative research and evaluation. For instance, it is worth posing the following questions related to a
completed evaluation:

- Did each fraction of the audience attend to the message?
- Did they understand it?
- Did they find it credible?
- Were the questions significant to them, answered as well as possible?
- Did the answers alter their preconceptions?
- Was the dialogue leading to decisions, enriched and elevated as a
  consequence of the evaluation?

MacDonald and Walker (1975) also argue that the data must be accessible to
the judgment and understanding of all those whose interests may be influenced by the contents.

However, the strength of these approaches is of an idealized rather than
practical nature. They depend upon a conception of audience as open and
sensitive, capable and unconstrained enough to explore the reconstructions of
reality presented them. Unfortunately, the everyday world for professional

workers is not so uncluttered. In *Opening and Closing* (1978), Klapp explores theories of openness and information use. He points out that systems of reception of information, be they individual or group, limit incoming information according to the system's self-regulatory need for balance or homeorhesis. New information is filtered into the system at rates which will allow assimilation and new order to form. It is a slow process. A natural opening and closing to new information which, with its inbuilt checks and balances preserves the constitution of the system. Institutions, committees and project or programme teams modulate this balanced flow towards gradual change through organizational structures and gatekeepers. The head of a school or division and the working party being fairly obvious examples. When information is too great or complex for the system to adjust to, Klapp calls it Social Noise. He makes three hypotheses about the problems of social noise which may particularly affect recipients of observation feedback.

- The greater the variety of signals. Messages, persons, purposes, viewpoints, cultures, mixing the higher is the potential for social noise.
- Tolerance for social noise decreases with strain, tension and fatigue.
- The load of social noise is high for gatekeepers and opinion leaders whose function is to transduce information rapidly or continually to a group depending upon them.

Within the product ranges of naturalistic evaluation there are obvious dangers here for case study and multiperspective reports which rely upon representing interview transcripts and observation notes to respondents and participants. The problem for naturalistic researchers is in how their objectives can be achieved in such a problematic context. What, in the nature of reportage are the characteristics which ensure that the evaluator's work services both the population under study and the greater population which may (or should) be informed, without this overload of social noise?

In *The Logic of Evaluative Argument* (1977), House, whilst defending argumentation against 'demonstration' in evaluation approaches, also emphasizes the need to address the particular user as opposed to the general on the basis that, the greater the perceived user population, then the more likely the attempt to satisfy will curtail the possibilities of discourse so that the work will devolve into pure deductive logic. In this he foreshadows the post-structuralist debate with its insistence on plays of difference, heterogeneity and idiosyncrasy. To escape the constraint of another form of logocentrism, evaluation needs to become 'persuasive' and thus, amenable to either rebuttal or interpretation in 'opening up of the text' for debate. Here, the text may be anything from fieldnotes, interview, observational notes and checklists to questionnaires and the final evaluation or research report. He concludes that the evaluator must engage his/her audiences in a dialogue in which they are free to employ their reasoning. This means that the audiences must assume personal responsibility for their interpretation of the evaluation since the reasoning presented to them is neither completely convincing nor entirely arbitrary.

While agreeing with this latter sentiment in principle, the premise that particular user-audiences will assume responsibility for evaluation or research writing and gain from it, is more than a little problematic. Exactly how effectively researchers and evaluators can feedback, formatively, what they have seen in notes, reports and case studies is open to debate. How feedback should be written to maximize its effects in raising consciousness about issues is a problem which has not yet been satisfactorily resolved in the discipline. But we make attempts at it. Here, for example, is a short extract from an evaluation report which tries to communicate the issues in pupils' choice-making at 16+. I wrote it as a diary a la Adrian Mole by Sue Townsend, so that teachers and students could have access to project reflections and recommendations.

> I looked at a poster display on what you need to be like to get a job. There was this unspotty youth and a pretty fifth form girl who both looked like they had been dressed by 'Next', him with his short hair and her with a page boy, preparing for their interviews. Honestly, there is no-one in our school looks like that. You'd think the place was a factory preparing kids to go into banking and insurance, looking at that stuff. My mate Jim is going to be a car mechanic like his Dad. He practically threw up over the smiling couple on the wall. (*The Secret Careers Diary of Craig (and Julie)*, Norfolk LEA, 1992)

In some ways this kind of writing is as problematic as academic writing, of course. It's very familiarity can smuggle a viewpoint through. But it attempts to represent the disenfranchised world of the young adult — and is open to criticism from that kind of reader, an individual who would quickly reject anything which appeared patronizing.

Essentially, this chapter addresses a particular kind of interface; that between the researcher and audiences, both within the population under study and beyond it. The medium which forms part of the connective tissue between the researcher's structuring of what is seen and participants' perceptions of the same, is a written product, a videotape, a film, or whatever. With these media there needs to be some deliberation upon the manner and form in which the evaluator feeds back to his users, these accounts of the 'field'. Deliberation on the problems of *significance* and *assimilation*.

That the problems of reporting in both formative and summative evaluative research remain largely undebated may be witnessed by any literature search. The position of Patten (1978) in an otherwise exhaustive study of the democratic possibilities of research-based evaluation as a *utilizable* process, is not unrepresentative, even today. Despite protocols, based on participant rights, there is little emphasis upon how to achieve an effective continuum of communication during the project or programme, or indeed, at the very end.

The reader will find very little in this book about what to do when a study is over. At that point the potential for utilization has been largely determined. Utilization-focussed evaluation emphasizes what happens in a study before a final report is produced. The key to utilization will be found on the path the evaluation takes before the findings are exposed to the general light of public scrutiny. (p. 21)

And at the conclusion of the book he remarks:

Brief executive summaries are more likely to be read than full reports. But most important, as with all other examples of utilization — focussed evaluation, the actual format, purpose and organization of the final report should be discussed and negotiated with identified decision makers and information users. (p. 266)

Whereas one can sympathize with the concerns behind these words I hope to show that the role of researcher or evaluator as reporter when engaged with the problems of impact, utilization and dissemination, needs overhauling in the light of research on audience cognition and its capacity to use information.

If House's conviction (and that of Barthes, Derrida, Foucault *et al*) is to be upheld that users must be free to interpret or deconstruct research and evaluation texts, then their penetration of, and playfulness with, the meanings within these texts, must be guaranteed. In other words, a suitable language must be sought which does not deny access and, therefore, levels of interpretation. On the other hand, it should be the wish of the evaluator or researcher that what is re-presented to an audience increases the possibility of discourse and enables it to act upon its interpretations, even, in Freire's terms, encouraging their *emancipation*. From House's particular audience to MacDonald's (1977) 'range of audiences', where the criterion of success is in the *range* of audiences served. He suggests that reporting should aspire to best-seller status. The key concepts of democratic evaluation are 'confidentiality', 'negotiation' and 'accessibility'. The key justificatory concept is 'the right to know'.

There is a strong, internal thread of agreement. Accessibility to the intended meanings of the researcher or evaluator's reporting is a precondition to its use or rejection in action. This may seen self-apparent and a basis for all styles of evaluative reporting, but, despite most authorities making passing note of it there is little account provided of what exactly should be the nature of the written or other interaction between the researcher and audience, how it can be refined and what characteristics are locatable within the formalized expression of research which enable users to act in the positive ways suggested by evaluators. Ways which ensure their own autonomy.

Later I will provide greater focus upon this problem area by developing the analogy of the relationship between homeopathy and allopathic medicine. However, for the moment, it would be more apposite to move on from the evaluators' preoccupation with stimulating professional and public discourse, either during a project or following the final report and reflect upon the nature of audiences. One thing is certain, in Lowry (1973) terms, the number of self-actualized and, therefore, ideal audience members is so small as to be disregardable! For instance, Maslow's idiosyncratic search for such individuals — a personal, empirical, iterative search — found that the vast majority of the human species confounded attempts to discover those who embody the characteristics of complete self-actualization.

It is, doubtless, to the vast *non-actualized* majority, that evaluation products are directed, which gives credibility to House's emphasis upon persuasion and argumentation. Audiences are comprised of individuals of every shade of opinion from reactionary to radical. In the main, people are not that easily converted or persuaded, except through exceptional circumstances to do so. What is the answer to audience resistance, then? How do researchers and evaluators 'break through' to the point where audiences engage in discourse?

Helen Simons' (1980) paper about case study presentations rather pragmatically conflates a desire for audience autonomy in decision-making with implications for the research report's circumnavigation of possible audience rejection of the data. She proposes that case study presentations should be basically *inconclusive* accounts of what happens in a particular professional setting and should contain accurate reports of the judgments, convergent or divergent, of those involved in the events.

On the other hand, material which confronts and threatens, whilst providing material for power bases to act against the individual or group, may do little to lift the intransigence of those whose activities are under scrutiny. It may have little educative value. If plural values and plural perspectives are to be considered and encouraged, then argumentation must be preferred to demonstration and discretion to confrontation.

Evaluation and other forms of research can represent various shades of power play ranging between the overly authoritarian and the democratically subordinate. It would be a fallacious conception to presume democratic tendencies in naturalist or qualitative research approaches, generally. Democracy is not, of course, generated by equal access and plural values per se; one ingredient which must make a researcher's work legitimately appropriate and democratic is its assimilability by all parties — including those beyond the allopathically named 'target population'. Just as witnesses before law are asked whether they understand the full import of their testimony, thereby legitimating the legal process, so research of all kinds should invoke similar safeguards. They are endorsed in the various principles and procedures which govern the use and ownership of information. However, language is so slippery that terms such as ownership of meaning or ownership of data are largely arbitrary, given the way they can be subjected to political forces. Even allowing for the indisputable fact that each reader may confirm his/her own perception of a piece of observation as fair and accurate, an interpretation informed by personal experience, doubts remain. So, when Roland Barthes (1977) says that it is impossible to write without labelling oneself, one is left with a sense of impasse: the evaluator as auteur proclaiming the rights of varied interpretations among the readership but, as likely as not, seen by the readership as integral to the framework of dominance: the paradoxical inheritance of the researcher as expert. Hood (1975) extends this line of argument when discussing the explicit and implicit powers of communicators in our society. The term is ironic in that communication tends to become distorted despite House's demand for the need for critical debate. The audience of the communicators plays the role of being both source and receiver:

> The process must still pass through the mediating structures of broad-casting itself — the broadcasts must select (and reject), transform into 'messages', (encode, develop formats, shape contents) — it is in and through that mediation — crucially for our purposes . . . that system-atic distortions enter the chain. (p. 119)

But we have seen that the raising of consciousness and the improvement of public discourse is a pronounced aim of researchers and evaluators. House's (1977) solution to this paradox has resonance. He suggests that groups of people adhere to opinion with variable intensity and that these beliefs should be put to the test of serious discourse. Even facts and values may be so considered. Rational discourse consists of giving reasons, although not com-pelling reasons. In the realm of action, where few things are clear and distinct, motivation can be rational. Practice can be reasonable. What we must be careful about, is going too far down this line. As Foucault (1989) says, exhor-tations to reason are, as often as not, the means by which the status quo is maintained.

It seems only part of the way to a solution. Where it stops short is in the blurred nature of the projected interaction between evaluator and user audi-ence. The shadow of scientific respectability is far-flung, hence the unfurling of the parasols of 'rationality' and 'reason'. Admission at the outset that the evaluator and researcher *are* interventive, whatever the checks and balances, and that one of their primary goals is to improve discourse, can lead to an interesting position. How does the interventive observer navigate through the rapids of a user's defensive rejection of his/her desire, the somewhat paternal-istic one of encouraging debate, whilst at the same time not prescribing or delimiting just such a debate?

Paulo Freire (1977) answers just such a dilemma by exhorting the use of what he terms 'generative themes'. Emancipation of the oppressed may come about by the joint action of investigators and oppressed (their audience) in co-investigation of these major themes.

He calls them generative because, however they are introduced and whatever action they may evoke, they contain the possibility of unfolding into again as many themes, which in their turn call for further investigation and reflection. The continual dialogue between these co-investigators uncovers limits to action and such discoveries afford the possibility of transcending those limits. How does this work in practice? Obviously, forms of action research can operate in exactly this way. But, at a day-to-day level, where researcher or evaluator are at work in the field, what guides the way that they communicate their observations to participants?

We return to the analogy of homeopathic medicine. Much of naturalistic research and evaluation, I would contend, is of an authoritarian nature and some quantitative evaluation is democratic. Whichever characterization one chooses depends entirely upon the assimilation and impact, take-up and understanding of observational products, whether they be field notes, interview transcripts, checklists or final reports. In allopathic medicine the doctor fights disease with whatever weapon is at hand — new drugs, operations, convulsion therapy — and the arena for this battle is the patient's body. There is little doubt that orthodox medicine is regarded as 'scientific' in much the way it was when leeches were applied and purgatives freely given. The essential nature of the treatment was to attack the illness directly and as speedily as possible. Despite the worn out cliché of 'the bedside manner' the medical profession is increasingly distancing itself from the patient in both human understanding and the technologization of its methodology. Patients become subsumed under disease headings. Despite the exceptions which give reason for hope, allopathy extends its empire into newer and more complex technology.

In homeopathic medicine (now accepted within the British National Health Service) the approach is different. Rather than this onslaught against the disease as a separate entity, the practitioner seeks to discover the complete picture of the patient's health — a form of case study rather than case history — and the treatment is not a 'cure' in the normally accepted sense, but is the provision of a substance which triggers off the body's own healing agencies (not such a bizarre concept considering recent medical research into endorphins). These substances are of such microscopic proportions as to be completely safe and free from any side-effects — so small, in fact, as to be regarded as absurdly dilute by conventional medicinal standards. To give a full picture of the way that allopathy and homeopathy contrast with each other is not the purpose here but a chart *may* help to point up the issue.

Let it be said that the homeopathic doctor will also carry a stomach pump and find use of allopathic treatments, particularly in certain life and death contexts. One approach doesn't completely negate the other. In conventional medicine, inoculations and vaccinations resemble the homeopathic art.

And now, back to handling observational data with, one hopes, a growing sense of analogy. The split into allopathy and homeopathy may clarify a model for an assimilable feedback process. In the handling and communication of observational data, allopathy encompasses those approaches and styles which involve the observer in a superordinate relationship with those whose activities s/he is observing, whether it be through the judgmental nature of intervention, through the invocation of the mysteries of the research profession or whether it be through the diminution and reification of living persons by conversion into statistics. It represents those interventions which, in the search

	ALLOPATHY	HOMEOPATHY
Advantages	aims for instant effect proof factor — double blind decisive marketable myth objective and rational	no side effects microscopic dose assimilation range of treatment possibility holistic appraisal interactive — democratic practitioner as colleague
Disadvantages	overkill side effects restricted targets for treatment treatment of symptoms/not causes impersonal/mechanistic authoritarian practitioner mystique	proof? validity slow acting indecisive irrational

for malfunction and its cure, do harm to part or all of the human network. Allopathy affirms pre-selected goals and narrow focus. It generates activity about symptoms and not causes. Allopathy would indicate the role of the observer as trouble-shooter and judge. Examples of these approaches and their outcomes can be found across a wide range of literature.

Within qualitative research approaches, allopathy would extend a sympathetic embrace to those who would adopt false consciousness, for this corresponds with the medical adage of 'doctor knows best'. It can find room for a raison d'etre which professes to brief decision makers for there is no danger here in separating person from mystique; and knowledge thus provided is raw material for established power bases. But at its root, and the reason it appeals to evaluative research concerned with 'condensed data gathering' (MacDonald and Walker, 1975), is its outsider, expert status, keen for quick dividends and fast appraisals. In this it adopts, in the affective areas of human relations, a stance which is almost oppositional and counteractive or paternalistic; there is an elemental requirement to change events, to correct imbalance, to project a therapy or offer a better way. The allopathic stance accords the observer with the status of consultant/healer.

The flow of activity and communication is from outside in, from evaluator to 'evaluatee' and is very different from the model of co-investigation developed by Freire. All this would not be said about homeopathic approaches. Nowhere here is heard, 'The operation was a great success but the patient died'. Indeed, where conventional medicine attempts to plug the hole in mortality, often prolonging suffering to a grotesque climax, there is evidence that homeopathy can allow a graceful and dignified exit from the world. The homeopathic doctor has no secret or mysterious arts. Treatment is based upon a catalogue of substances known to cause symptoms similar to the vast range that the body can produce. These 'poisons' — Paracelsus said in the sixteenth century that all things are poisons, for there is nothing without a poisonous quality, it is only the dose which makes a thing a poison — are pharmaceutically prepared in incredibly dilute forms and when given to the patient can effect a cure over a period. Where there *is* mystery and scepticism from the orthodoxy, is in how the administration of such small doses can cause the body to heal itself. There is an interesting parallel here with the clamour for scientific proof of the effectiveness of naturalistic approaches, an equivalent to the medical 'double-blind' validity check, and consequent naturalistic defences of 'shock of recognition' or 'the provision of vicarious experience'. (Stake, 1975) But, in homeopathic evaluation, the doses so to speak, are provided in the forms of fragments of spoken interaction, reports, portrayals, interviews, video-tapes or photographs and are so framed that they may be assimilated by the individual or group and, upon assimilation, reflection may occur which empowers the audience take action. And, as Abercrombie (1979) would argue, audiences become better decision-makers as a result of reflected experiences and their recognition of 'truths' in evaluative research material.

It is the contention here that the homeopathic approach explores as much of the context as need be grasped within the hermeneutic circle suggested earlier, thus building an interleaved structure of plural perspectives to constitute the 'dose'. It is the composition of doses which is critical for they must closely resemble events in a particular way. Rather as the holographic plate, when splintered, produces fragments which contain the whole image of the intact plate (see Shotter and Newson, 1980; and Bohm, 1980) and the human organism defines the nature of the poison from a benign pilule with its poisonous echoes (the homeopathic dose), forms of feedback from the evaluator must have metonymic qualities. That is, these forms of feedback must contain sufficient representation of the structure of events for these events to be meaningfully recreated by recipients and must also be small enough to be non-threatening whilst potent enough to stimulate discourse. In these powerful microforms, be they metaphorical, enigmatic, representational or symbolic, the research or evaluator embarks on a journey of hope, to create discourse. They become evaluation's own generative themes. It may well be that those evaluators such as Day and Stake (1978) and Pick and Walker (1976) who vouchsafe or demonstrate the use of anecdotes and vignettes began to realize their power as stimulants of discourse. These authors describe vignettes as small illustrations or perhaps facets of an issue, only suggestive, but poignant. They will often comprise a wisp of a dialogue but sometimes grow beyond the size of anecdote to become a short story. It may be the trace of previous action, 'such as the smudge of lip prints on a photograph'. Momentarily it is 'figure', but shades off into the larger meaning of the issue, the 'group'. Here, the connection with Roland Barthes' punctum (1982), discussed in chapter 3, becomes obvious.

For the analogy to become a working hypothesis, it requires that each individual be regarded as the organism (or hermeneutic circle) whilst also helping to comprise other, larger group organisms (also hermeneutic circles). The observer, as hermeneutic practitioner, co-investigates through social interaction based upon low key, sympathetic responsiveness, the media and networks which help determine the cohesion of the organism. Once sufficiently inside the circle s/he must set about the problem of representing understandings of what is being experienced, in non-judgmental, yet potent forms and thereby setting up the unfolding of themes and action as Freire suggests in *Pedagogy of the Oppressed.* Observation becomes part of an interactive continuum, heightened by the transitory presence of the observer.

Postscript

How is this borne out in practice?

In some of the earliest research I ever did, I observed ten teachers working in classrooms. I was looking for evidence of the transmission of complex concepts within the pedagogical. When I came to negotiate clearance of pieces of transcript, or showed how I would quote from the experience, I was struck by how much individuals pored over and got out of such small samples. They could generate a half-hour conversation from a few lines of dialogue. Why? I think that by selecting these small details from the collages of events, the researcher is saying that this stands as a potent metonym for the rest, or at least for some major issue or concern. The reader assimilates this crumb and begins to recreate what the cake is like. For example by including an example of a particular teacher cutting across a student's reply within a piece dealing ostensibly with the elaboration of a difficult concept, I found that I had unwittingly given that teacher enough information to rethink an entire strategy of interaction.

Within an MSc course in Education and Training at my institution, the use of real commissions serves to initiate students into the exigencies of research practice. These short commissions provide public and private organizations with (non-threatening) researchers for brief (three to four weeks) periods after which short reports are fed back to the sponsors of the research. Everyone is aware of the problems of time and inexperience but some of the results have been quite startling.

What I am suggesting is that it is not necessary to describe the full current of a person or group's participation in events, but rather to choose, judiciously, small details which are representative of action. Whole transcripts of taped interviews remain opaque, intimidating and over bulky for most, whereas selected extracts are pithier and more appropriate for consideration, and provide illumination of possible usage whilst encouraging further reflection, dialogue and co-investigation. The skill and concern of the observer is in measuring the dose, comprehending its potency and in then accepting the unpredictability of the way such knowledge may be used. The observer becomes not only a broker of information between parties who want to know, but a broker of dialogues among those who are interested.

12 Tales of Future Past

There is in fact no insoluble waste problem. The problem is resolved by the post-modern invention of recycling and the incinerator. The great incinerators of history, from whose ashes the Phoenix of post-modernity is resuscitated! We have come to terms with the idea that everything that was not degradable or exterminable is today recyclable, and hence there is no final solution. We shall not be spared the worst — that is, history will not come to an end — since the leftovers, all the leftovers — the Church, communism, ethnic groups, conflicts, ideologies — are infinitely recyclable. What is stupendous is that nothing one thought superseded by history has really disappeared. All the archaic, anachronistic forms are there, ready to emerge, intact and timeless, like the viruses deep in the body. History has only wrenched itself from cyclical time to fall into the order of the recyclable. (Baudrillard, 1994, p. 27)

This quotation comes from Baudrillard's, *The Illusion of the End*. In many ways it serves to illuminate the thesis of this book, that observational research is used to document the fermentation of the recycled. It operates as the gloved hand of ideology, masking its likeness to the body. It offers openness with spread fingers in apparent supplication. It is used by the powerful to subordinate the weak and by the fifth cavalry to emancipate the downtrodden. The observer floats like a torn scrap of text upon the turbulences, Baudrillard describes.

There are lots of Jack Sangers in this book, literally upholding Barthes' famous declaration concerning the death of the author. They have come and gone from different periods of my researching life and only some have the same name. The 'self' or amalgam of selves has changed, sometimes dramatically, over time. There are also all the other voices represented here; previous authors, respondents, participants. In some ways the book is fractured and discontinuous. In many ways it is very partial. What I hope it does, despite these failings, is help along the debate about being an observer in research. Since it is autobiographical, it is idiosyncratic but it tries to depict the various ways that I have tried to work with the insoluble, the complex and the challenging. Somewhere in it, there is an attempt to offer practical advice. Then again, that very advice is challenged in other parts . . .

To sum up, I have tried to focus attention upon observation, a largely undebated activity within social science research.

And what of the future? Of what will observation consist? Where are we going? I'd like to draw together various threads to speculate upon this theme; technology, post-structuralist perspectives and social change. And I'd like to start with a photograph from a project that I am directing as this book emerges. If you want to engage in my language game, look at the following image and think what it tells you as a researcher.

Presented with this photograph, what do you say? How do you interpret it? Well, you could count the various bits of information under category headings such as board games, soft toys, video games, videos. You could make a bald statement about consumerism and how children have so much in their possession. You could say that the photograph is an example of late twentieth century acquisitiveness. In other words you would use the photograph as a means to *illustrate* your thesis. It would be evidence for your thesis. In some way or another, the thesis would be antecedent and the photograph subsequent and part of the corpus of material which binds together the thesis.

However, there is another way of using this evidence. We find its genesis in chapter 3, in the exposition on Roland Barthes' *Camera Lucida.* Barthes talks of each photograph being a mathesis singularis, a phenomenological entity in itself, its own corpus of knowledge. Whilst this can create unease on the part of the observer-interpreter used to the solidity and security of the embrace of theory, it can also be liberating. Rather than trying to interpret the photograph in terms of an existing theoretical perspective, the *reader* is released into authorship. That is, s/he is liberated to make novel responses to the 'text' of the image, knowing full well that others may see it differently but that a richer discourse is developed from this heterogeneity of responses. And now to my own response:

> It's a child's bedroom of today. Precisely 1993. In another month or two, the titles below the bottom shelf will change. It's an example of a bedroom as a retail outlet. Louis, as consumer/user, stands as if before a shop window. His toys are divided by the shelves. The past, represented by the legs of soft toys, reach down, across the barrier of the top shelf, as though trying to draw him back into his younger years. The future lies below the barrier of the bottom shelf, half in darkness, dragging him away from such soft entreaties. Video titles sit here waiting in their neat piles. Louis' world is neatly trisected. The present, signified by the middle section, contains board games, activities demanding the physical presence of others. Yet, even at its heart, heralding the world below its own surface, this section frames the tautology, OPTIC VISION. So we pan down the photograph and we see the three ages of Louis. Cuddly toys implying tactility, intimacy and dependency. Games that demand being with others in varying degrees of contact. Then, the separation into sole viewer, sole user.

Hang on a minute — is this research writing? It is hardly permissible according to any of the traditional standards of research. It is off the wall. What we are asked to accept is that evidence constitutes a flux of possibilities that roll around each other forming new meanings with each new set of contacts and juxtapositions. This evidence is then convenience-packed like fast food, in new shapes with new constituents, tailored to meet the reader's requirements. Quite so. But what gives it an extra twist, throwing the process in the air so that it falls about us like Alice's courtroom, is that the photographic image, is itself prey to the same procedures. My research photograph is authentic enough, in the every day sense. But photographs are now encoded on disks and wired to the editor's office. They are merely so many digitized dots which can be reformed in any way that the editor chooses. The evidence can be produced to illuminate the story.

Enervating it may be for some, it is extraordinarily energizing for others. The hidden social constructions of reality of the past become the explicit constructions of the present. The grand narratives of research, which help to form our mythologies about society, give way to these individualized interpretations of the world.

Is this hugely individualized interaction possible? Of course. It is called the INTERNET. The stupefying knowledge that there is a greater number of connections possible between neurones in the brain, than there are lumps of matter in the universe becomes projected on to this system of communication. Millions of individuals can currently talk to millions of other individuals, the whole system becoming a symbolized reconstruction of what happens inside a single individual's brain. As the INTERNET, itself, gives way to more sophisticated communications, the whole/part complexity becomes ever more complex.

Since observation is, more than anything else, focused communication, what will be its role in this grave new world? These mediated realities? I began to write about mediated realities, as an educational issue in the late 1980s. Here is my thinking from that time.

Mediation is a concept not particularly scrutinized in the investigation of classrooms, yet its significance becomes very apparent in a technological era. Given that pupils' lives up to the mid-1950s tended to have a more direct relation to the physical world, what has gradually happened since is that such biographies have contained a greater and greater proportion of mediated experience. Television, radio, photographic reproductions, gramophones, cassettes, videos and cinema have gradually combined to provide a permanent, artificial mirror (through which we might, like Alice, escape) to our lives. To this, in the last few years, has been added the microcomputer.

Essentially there has been a proliferation of data which, if we follow the thinking of semiologists, break down into three distinct groups: icons, indices and symbols. The groups move progressively from the concrete to the abstract.

In a primary school a child might look at pictures of 'the hand' in a book; an iconic representation. It might draw around the hand and the silhouette would be an indexical representation. It might measure the hand with Cuisenaire rods and produce a symbolic representation (or write the word 'hand').

These are all levels of mediation. The hand becomes gradually transfigured and then transformed until it is represented in a completely abstract symbol or set of symbols.

Most of what a pupil is presented with at school is mediated in some way, by pictures and by language (orally or written). Classrooms, as the child matures, are increasingly less tactile environments. They are increasingly containers in which concepts, or the arrangement of symbols, take the place of the direct apprehension of the world. Observing classrooms makes one aware of artificiality. The relations between individuals, the sets and subsets of rules, implicit and explicit, the stuff of the curriculum and the manner of its delivery gradually erode direct experience. There is a curious paradox in the educational computer technologist insisting upon 'hands-on' experience as a way of comprehending the machine as tool and toy rather than tyrant. Mere handson experience does not enable the pupil to comprehend the binary operations which transform reality into a million switches in the hardware and the resultant images upon the screen.

Information handling is, largely, the handling of mediated experience, not the handling of persons and things directly. The better the pupil can handle the transformation of reality the more she or he is rewarded. The less 'real' — that is, fully apprehended and directly affected by personal pupil and teacher intervention the easier it is to package the curriculum in classrooms and the more difficult it is for more pupils to engage in classroom processes.

Metacognition, through the channel of critique, is perhaps the only way in which artificiality is exposed and mediational operations become understood. Language is used to subvert its own obfuscations. The logical distancing of the pupil from reality has to be deconstructed to reach the prize of understanding, the premises and bases upon which information has been constructed. To evolve critique, the pupil or student (and teacher) may need to be allowed to 'play' with the curriculum. To treat it as clay rather than Lego.

In the following example (from Tom Logan's fieldnotes, a co-researcher of that time) a pupil 'breaks through' the mirror of a film. Other pupils are treating the medium in the receptive way they have become accustomed to. That is, they are receiving the data, without critique, and are unlikely to be engaged in the informing process at any deep level.

Alan is 12 and, quite frankly, a pain. The sort of lad whose hand always goes up to answer quick as a flash, and is almost always wrong. Not even the sort of wrong where you can say 'Not bad' or 'Close', or even 'Good try' but so off-beam that he has obviously not understood. Depending on how far off he is the rest of the group consider it entertainment (laughs) or tedium (groans). It is perhaps the inevitability which is most disheartening. There are always ways of pretending you don't see his hand waving under your nose, in order to quickly ask someone else who might know, to save his (your?) embarrassment. But when no-one in the group knows — Alan's hand is in solo flight. And his answers on those occasions usually involve a fantasy beginning with an uncle, often not living locally, sometimes even a war-hero, who told him 'the answer'. Way off-beam — in fact the group reaction never allowing the answer to emerge from the daydream.

The real problem is that we're half-way through our second-term together and he's getting worse, not better. He's now becoming a self-constructed clown/victim, presumably on the basis of any attention being better than none. Talking to the remedial teacher makes me more sympathetic — he is withdrawn from his tutor group during their 'normal' English and maths — but left in for science, French and integrated studies. Help!

Whilst demonstrating the system/syllabus imbalance and the lack of individual pastoral care a revelatory classroom incident reveals his potential (that we all know is in there in theory). After watching a film on 'animal behaviour' in which the underlying teacher strategy is pupil observation and question-posing — in itself a switch of tactics — Alan's behaviour is suddenly normalized. Many 'right-answer' children ask off-beam questions, seemingly based on guessing what teacher wants from them rather than on what they have seen and want to inquire about. Alan on the other hand isn't guessing, does base his questions on what he sees, does, now, know how to ask in order to understand:- 'Why do elephants feed their young at the front, like humans, not at the back like — like animals?

After the habitual laughter, the seriousness of the question becomes felt. None of us had noticed. A quick rewind of the film proves he is right — they do! Alan, the best observer, seeing what is there, the rest of us looking through our conventionalised categories. We have no answer — so Alan goes off to find the biology teacher 'expert', who sends him to the library. The librarian sends him back with a note of the Teachers Centre phone number. The Teachers Centre warden searches. Comes into school the next day. She and Alan write and type a letter to the British Zoological Society, Regents Park (London Zoo to us). A letter arrives from the B.Z.S. Research Officer, praising Alan's observational powers, and informing us of the particular branch of the evolutionary tree (the dead end) that the elephant shares with a small furry creature called a tock hyrax. Apart from humans, Alan later discovers from the warden, only the dugong or manatee also feed 'at the front'. They also feed upright, sometimes sitting on rocks, and may have led to the stories about mermaids from early American sailors, long away at sea. His project folder becomes a star attraction.

The point is that Alan is not just a temporary hero. He became a respected member of a questioning group. We even listened to the stories about his uncles, and given time, they had a point. Question-posing was now insisted upon, and teacher-impositional guessing games became old hat.

Perhaps the moral of this story is about initiating the enquiry. Handling the information. Learning. (And perhaps teaching others a thing or two.)

In the preceding example the pupil subverts the compelling power of the images on a **film** to make information 'real' to him. Classrooms have gloss. They can become equally unreal as pupils and staff fall into ritual and established role. Examples of how pupils can be encouraged to deconstruct these inevitably constraining patterns can be found in many of the teachers papers in part 2. In Maxine Wood's paper on marking, 7- and 8-year-olds begin to penetrate the mediated relationship they have with the teacher. The reality of the people behind the assessing relationship is drawn into the foreground.

Information handling must not be seen in one garb only. In the way it is taught or included in schools generally, it has an ethos much like international trade. Information is a commodity which is exported and imported and is valued according to its rarity or importance. In such a guise it is denuded of personal relevance and intersubjective impact. It becomes a medium of factuality. For the pupil it can become mediated to such a degree that it loses any coherence as something vital for his/her future survival in society. There is no way for pupils to create it, transmute it and own it.

In the time which has elapsed since this was written, the INTERNET has arrived and the possibilities of young people making, owning, transferring, receiving and exploring information been revolutionized. As with all of us. We can all be Alans. Baudrillard's dustbin of history can be ransacked for new ideas from the old. But, equally, the novel and the revolutionary can find a hearing '*Somewhere out there, someone waits for me*', says the song.

But this active engagement with others is in symbolic space. Hackers are caught, regularly, in places they should not be. They are bandit ethnographers, seeking to illuminate strange cultures. The wanderers on the INTERNET might meet in London at the Cybercafe, like dinosaurs from Edwardian social conventions, but, in the main, they prefer not to. Why be locked into the persona you carry around all day and night? Better the ghostly world where you can play with pictures of who you might want to be at any particular second. And your ghostly selves can play with others' ghostly selves in an infinite change of self-signification. Recently I sat on Anglia Polytechnic University's Research Degrees Committee and we discussed a research proposal concerning the mapping of this cyberspace, this symbolic ground where mediated souls come and go, materialize and vanish. The subject area for the research was geography! The research method chosen to examine the phenomenon was ethnography!

As we have seen, observation in research involves acts of mediation because accounts are rendered of what is seen. Whether written, recorded, spoken, filmed or photographed, they are reconstructions from a particular perspective. And in future this gradual movement from oral feedback to video tape, will extend further into the realms of virtual reality, holograms and cyberspace. Virtual reality is a term for quasi-reality, computer modelled other world, as near to our own as can be achieved. In such modelled worlds, already, NATO tests out proposed battle strategies against Iraq, or whoever the purported transgressor. In the recent war with Iraq, it was suggested that some military staff, operating computer controlled simulated realities in the desert in the US did not know that they were engaged in real war in real time. A consultant eye surgeon friend tells em that with robots and computer links, operations can be carried out by the surgeon, several thousand miles from the patient.

One can envisage packages which are robust virtual populations, ready to be tested by market researchers. On INTERNET there could be whole environments encoded on CD ROM, available for the observer to investigate schools, hospitals, homes and offices. In time, the observers themselves will be replaced by error free virtual robot analysts. The cyborgs will populate mediated, symbolic space. And where will our realities be then?

What is ethnography if it isn't forever patrolling the frontiers of flesh and blood, seeking to illuminate what it is to be human and providing the means by which we see ourselves in the process of change, reminding us of how much we are culpable when we abrogate our responsibilities for others and ourselves.

Postscript

One of the best-known Hollywood legends concerns the final scene of *Casablanca*. It is said that even during the shooting itself, the director and writers oscillated between different versions of the denouement (Ingrid Bergman leaves with her husband; she stays with Bogart; one of the two men dies). Like most such legends this one is false, one of the ingredients of the myth of *Casablanca* constructed afterward (in reality, there were some discussions about possible endings, but they were resolved well before the shooting), but it nevertheless illustrates perfectly how the 'quilting point' (point de capiton) functions in a narration. We experience the present ending (Bogart sacrifices his love and Bergman leaves with her husband) something that 'naturally' and 'organically' follows from the preceding action, but if we were to imagine another ending — say, for example, that Bergman's heroic husband were to die and that Bogart were to take his place on the plane for Lisbon together with Bergman — it, too, would be experienced by viewers as something that developed 'naturally' out of earlier events. How is this possible, given that the earlier events are the same in both cases? The only answer is, of course, that the experience of a linear 'organic' flow of events is an illusion (albeit a necessary one) that masks the fact that it is the ending that retroactively confers the consistency of an organic whole on the preceding events. What is masked is the radical contingency of the enchainment of narration, the fact that, at every point, things might have turned out otherwise. But if this illusion is a result of the very linearity of the narration, how can the radical contingency of the enchainment of events be made visible? The answer is, paradoxically, by proceeding in a reverse way, by presenting the events backwards from the end to the beginning. Far from being just a hypothetical solution, this procedure has been put in to practice several times. (Zizek, 1991, p. 69)

Bibliography

ABERCROMBIE, M.L.J. (1979) *The Anatomy of Judgement*, Harmondsworth, Penguin.
APULEIUS (1980) *The Golden Ass*, Harmondsworth, Penguin.
BALL, S. (1981) *Beachside Comprehensive*, London, Cambridge University Press.
BARTHES, R. (1964) *Image Music Text*, (trans. S Heath) London, Fontana.
BARTHES, R. (1977) *Writing Degree Zero*, New York, Hill and Wang.
BARTHES, R. (1982) *Camera Lucida*, London, Jonathon Cape.
BARTHES, R. (1984) *Image Music Text*, London, Fontana.
BAUDRILLARD, J. (1994) *The Illusion of the End*, Oxford, Polity Press.
BECKER, H. (1967) 'Whose side are we on?', *Social Problems*, **14**, pp. 239–47.
BENNETT, W.L. and FELDMAN, M. (1981) *Reconstructing Reality in the Courtroom*, London, Tavistock.
BHASKAR, R. (1975) *A Realist Theory of Science*, Leeds, Leeds Books.
BHASKAR, R. (1979) 'On the possibility of social scientific knowledge and the the limits of naturalism', *Journal of the Theory of Social Behaviour*, **8**, 1, pp. 1–28.
BLUMER, H. (1969) *Symbolic Interactionism*, Englewood Cliffs, NJ, Prentice Hall.
BOHM, D. (1980) *Wholeness and the Implicate Order*, London, Routledge and Kegan Paul.
BOHM, D. and PLEAT, D.F. (1988) *Science, Order and Creativity*, London, Routledge and Kegan Paul.
BROWN, G. (1984) *Microteaching*, London, Methuen.
BURGESS, R. (1992) 'Linking design and analysis in ethnographic studies', paper presented to the annual meeting of the British Educational Research Association, Stirling University.
CARR, W. and KEMMIS, S. (1983) *Becoming critical: Knowing through Action Research*, London, Falmer Press.
CICOUREL, A.V. and KITSUSE, J.I. (1963) *Decision Makers*, New York, Bobbs-Merrill.
COHEN, D.K. and GARET, M.S. (1975) 'Reforming educational policy with applied research', *Harvard Educational Review*, **43**, 1.
COHEN, R.S. and WARTOFSKY, L. (1983) *Epistemology, Methodology and Social Sciences*, New York, Reidel.
COMTE, A. (1978) *Introduction to Postive Philosophy*, San Franscio, Hackett.
CRONBACH, L.J. (1975) 'Beyond the two disciplines of scientific psychology', *American Psychologist*, February.

CULLER, J. (1976) *Saussure*, London, Fontana.

DAY, J.A. and STAKE, R. (1978) 'Research methods used' in *Case Studies in Science Education Booklet 0*, Centre for Instructional Research and Curriculum Evaluation and Committee on Culture and Cognition, University of Illinois at Urbana-Champaign.

DEIKMAN, A.J. (1982) *The Observing Self*, Boston, MA, Beacon Press.

DERRIDA, J. (1976) *Of Grammatology*, Baltimore, MD, Johns Hopkins University Press.

DERRIDA, J. (1978) *Writing and Difference*, London, Routledge.

DICKEY, B. (1980) 'Utilization of evaluation of small-scale innovative educational projects', *Educational Evaluation and Policy Analysis*, November–December, **2**, 6.

DOCKER, J. (1994) *Post-modernism and Popular Culture*, Cambridge, Cambridge University Press.

EAGLETON, T. (1983) *Literary Theory: An Introduction*, Oxford, Blackwell.

EISNER, E. (1972) 'Emerging models for educational evaluation', *Social Review 1971–1972*, **80**, pp. 573–90.

ELLIOTT, J. (1985) 'Educational action research', in NISBETT, T. *et al* (Eds) *World Year Book of Education*, London, Kogan Page, pp. 231–50.

EMPSON, W. (1930) *Seven Types of Ambiguity*, London, Penguin.

FORD, T. (1975) *Unit 1 Patterns of Teaching, Unit 2 Research Methods Unit 3 Hypotheses Unit 4 Teacher Case Studies*, Cambridge, Cambridge Institute of Education.

FOUCAULT, M. (1974) *The Order of Things*, London, Tavistock/Routledge.

FOUCAULT, M. (1980) *Power and Knowledge: Selected Interviews and Other Writings 1972–77* (Ed C. Gordon), New York, Pantheon.

FOUCAULT, M. (1989) *The Order of Things: An Archaeology of the Human Sciences*, London, Routledge.

FOX, T. and HERNANDEZ-NIETO, R. (1981) 'Why not quantitative methodologies to illuminate dialectical or phenomenological perspectives?', paper presented to the annual meeting of the American Educational Research Association, April 1977.

FREIRE, P. (1977) *Pedagogy of the Oppressed*, Harmondsworth, Penguin.

GADAMAR, H.G. (1975) *Truth and Method*, London, Sheed and Ward.

GARFINKEL, H. (1964) 'Studies in the routine grounds of every day activities', *Social Problems*, **11**, pp. 225–50.

GAULD, S. and SHOTTER, J. (1977) *Human Action and Its Psychological Investigation*, London, Routledge and Kegan Paul.

GIDDENS, A. (1976) *New Rules in Sociological Method*, London, Hutchinson.

GIDDENS, A. (1979) *Central Problems in Social Theory*. London, Macmillan.

GIDDENS, A. (1982) *Profiles and Critiques in Social Theory*, London, MacMillan.

GIDDENS, A. (1991) *Sociology*, Cambridge, Polity Press.

GLASER, B. and STRAUSS, A. (1967) *The Discovery of Grounded Theory*, New York, Aldine.

GLEICK, J. (1987) *CHAOS*, London, Cardinal.

GOMBRICH, E.H. (1994) *Meditations on a Hobby Horse and the Other Essays on the Theory of Art*, London, Phaidon.

GORDON, C. *et al* (1980) 'Foucault: Power/Knowledge: Selected Interviews and Other Writings 1972–1977', Bright, The Harvester Press.

GOULDNER, A.W. (1968) 'The sociologist as partisan', *American Sociologist*, May.

GRIFFITHS, M. (1995) 'Feminism, post-modernism and educational research', *British Educational Research Journal*, **21**, 2, pp. 219–35.

GUBA, E. and LINCOLN, Y. (1981) *Effective Evaluation*, London, Jossey Bass.

HABERMAS, J. (1971) *Knowledge and Human Interests*, Boston, MA, Beacon Press.

HABERMAS, J. (1972) *Knowledge and Human Interests*, London, Heinemann.

HABERMAS, J. (1974) *Theory and Practice*, London, Heineman.

HAMMERSLEY, M. and ATKINSON, P. (1983) *Ethnography: Principles in Practice*, London, Tavistock.

HARGREAVES, D. (1967) *Social Relations in the Secondary School*, London, Routledge and Kegan Paul.

HARRE, R. and SECORD, P.F. (1972) *The Explanation of Social Behaviour*, Oxford, Blackwell.

HAWKING, S. (1988) *A Brief History of Time*, London, Bantam.

HERRIGEL, E. (1972) *Zen in the Art of Archery*, London, Routledge and Kegan Paul.

HOODS, S. (1975) 'The structured communication of events', *Getting the Message Across*, UNESCO Press.

HOUSE, E. (1977) *The Logic of Evaluative Argument*, Centre for the Study of Evaluation, Los Angeles, University of California.

HUGHES, P. and BRECHT, G. (1976) *Vicious Circles and Infinity*, London, Cape.

HUSSERL, E. (1964) *The Paris Lectures*, (trans. Keostenbaum P.), The Hague, Martinus Nijhoff.

JACKSON, P. (1968) *Life in Classrooms*, New York, Holt Rinehart and Winston.

JOHNSON, J.M. (1974) *Doing Fieldwork Research*, London, Collier MacMillan.

KATZ, E. (1975) 'The mass communication of knowledge' in *Getting the Message Across*, UNESCO Press.

KLAPP, O. (1978) *Opening and Closing*, Cambridge, Cambridge University Press.

KOESTLER, A. (1989) *The Act of Creation*, London, Hutchinson.

KUHN, T. (1970) *The Structure of Scientific Revolutions*, Chicago, IL, Chicago University Press.

KYRIACOU, C. (1990) 'Establishing the trustworthiness of naturalistic studies', *Research Intelligence*, summer, **36**.

LACAN, J. (1994) *The Four Fundamental Concepts of Psycho-Analysis*, London, Penguin.

LACEY, C. (1970) *Hightown Grammar*, Manchester, Manchester University Press.

LOWRY, R. (Ed) (1973) *Dominance, Self Esteem, Self Actualization-Germinal Papers of A.H. Maslow*, California, Brooks Cole Publishing Company.

MACDONALD, B. (1976) 'Evaluation and the control of education', in TAWNEY, D. (Ed) *Curriculum Evaluation Today: Trends and Implications*, Schools Council Research Studies, London, MacMillan Education.

MACDONALD, B. (1977) 'A political classification of evaluation studies', in

HAMILTON, D. *et al* (Eds) *Beyond the Numbers Game*, London, MacMillan Education.

MacDonald, B. (1978) 'Democracy and Evaluation', public address to the University of Alberta, Faculty of Education, Edmonton, October 1979.

MacDonald, B. (1980) 'Mandarins and lemons', presented at an AERAL symposium entitled 'Case Study in Policy Evaluation: Paradoxes of Popularity' in Los Angeles, Norwich, CARE, University of East Anglia.

MacDonald, B. and Sanger, J. (1982) 'Just for the record: Notes towards a theory of interviewing in evaluation', in House, E. (Ed) *Evaluation Studies Review Annual* Vol. 7, Beverley Hills, CA, Sage.

MacDonald, B. and Walker, R. (1975) 'Case study and the social Philosophy of educational research', *Cambridge Journal of Education*, **5**, 11, Lent.

Michel, J. (1973) *A View over Atlantis*, London, Paladin.

Moustakis, C. (1990) *Heuristic Research*, London, Sage.

Norris, C. (1987) *Derrida*, London, Fontana.

Norris, N. and Sanger, J. (1984) *Inside Information: An Evaluation of a Curriculum Innovation*, Norwich, UEA Occasional Publications.

Parlett, M. and Hamilton, D. *et al* (1977) *Beyond the Numbers Game*, London, MacMillan.

Patten, M.Q. (1978) *Utilization Focussed Evaluation*, California, Sage Publications.

Phillips, A. (1994) *On Flirtation*, London, Faber and Faber.

Pick, C. and Walker, R. (1976) 'Other rooms other voices', *Ford Safari Project*, Norwich, CARE, University of East Anglia.

Polanyi, M. (1969) 'Knowing and being', in Grene, M. (Ed) *Knowing and Being — Essays by Michael Polanyi*, Chicago, IL, Chicago University Press.

Popper, K.R. (1972) *The Logic of Scientific Discovery*, London, Hutchinson.

Price, G.G. (1981) 'Quantification and curriculum research: Red herrings and real vices', paper presented at the annual meeting of the American Educational Research Association, Los Angeles.

Reichenbach, H. (1938) *Experience and Prediction: An Analysis of the Foundations and the Structure of Knowledge*, Chicago, IL, University of Chicago Press.

Reinhartz, S. (1988) 'Feminist distrust: Problems of context and content in sociological work', in Berg, D. and Smith, K.K. (Eds) *The Self in Social Enquiry*, London, Sage.

Rorty, R. (1991) *Objectivity, Relativism, and Truth*, Cambridge, Cambridge University Press.

Rouse, J. (1994) 'Power/knowledge', in Cutting, G. (Ed) *The Cambridge Companion to Foucault*, Cambridge, Cambridge University Press.

Sanger, J. (1985) 'Data into knowledge: A basis for analysing information handling in classrooms', *Cambridge Journal of Education*, **15**, 2, pp. 67–73.

Sanger, J. (1986) 'Natural options in evaluation reporting', paper presented at the annual meeting of the American Educational Research Association, San Francisco.

Sanger, J. (1989a) *Teaching, Handling Information and Learning*, Boston Spa, British Library Publications.

SANGER, J. (1989b) 'The Sick Fly' in *Classroom Processes*, Deakin University.

SANGER, J. (1990) 'Awakening a scream of consciousness: The critical group in action research', *Theory into Practice*, **XXIX**, 3, pp. 174–8.

SANGER, J. (1991) *The Norfolk LEA Staying On Rates Project: The Final Report 1991*, Norwich, Norfolk Educational Press.

SANGER, J. (1992) 'Changing the teaching ethos', paper presented at the annual meeting of the British Education Research Association, Stirling University.

SANGER, J. (1993) *Entertainment Technology and the Young Learner*, London, British Film Institute.

SANGER, J. (1995a) 'Five easy pieces', *BERA Journal*, **21**, 1.

SANGER, J. (1995b) 'Making action research mainstream: A post-modern perspective on appraisal', *Educational Action Research: An International Journal*, **3**, 1.

SANGER, J. (1995c) in ZUBER-SKERRIT, O. (Ed) *Managing Change through Action Research: A Post-modern Perspective or Appraisal*, forthcoming.

SANGER, J. and SCHOSTAK, J. (1981) *Carrying off the Case* Norwich, CARE, University of East Anglia.

SCHUTZ, A (1967) 'Common sense and scientific interpretation of human action' in *Collected Papers, Vol 1*, The Hague, Martinus Nijhoff.

SHOTTER, J. and NEWSON, J. (1980) 'An ecological approach to cognitive development: Implicate orders, joint action and intentionality', in BUTTERWIRTH, S. and LIGHT, P. (Eds) *The Individual and the Social in Cognitive Development*, Brighton, Harvester Press.

SIMONS, H. (1971) 'Innovation and the case study of school', *Cambridge Journal of Education No. 3*, Michaelmass Term.

SIMONS, H. (1980) 'Negotiating conditions for independent evaluations' (mimeo) Curriculum Studies Department, University of London Institute of Education.

SMITH, L.M. (1981) 'An evolving logic of participant observation, educational ethnography and other case studies', in SHULMAN, L. (Ed) *Review of Research in Education*, Chicago, IL, Peacock.

SMITH, L.M. and GEOFFREY, W. (1968) *The Complexities of an Urban Classroom*, New York, Holt Rinehart and Winston.

STAKE, R.E. (Ed) (1975) *Evaluating the Arts in Education: A Responsive Approach*, Columbus, OH, C.E. Merrill.

STENHOUSE, L. (1975) *Introduction to Curriculum Research and Design*, London, Heinemann.

STRAUSS, A. and CORBIN, J. (1991) *The Basics of Qualitative Research*, London, Sage.

THOMAS, W.I. (1919) *The Polish Peasant in Europe and America*, Boston, Richard B. Badger.

TOULMIN, S. (1972) *Human Understanding*, Oxford, Clarendon Press.

ULMER, G. (1985) *Applied Grammatology*, New York, John Hopkins.

VERNON, M.D. (1970) *The Psychology of Perception*, London, Penguin.

WALKER, R. (1982) 'The use of fiction in educational research (and I don't mean

Cyril Burt)', in Sᴍᴇᴛʜᴇʀʜᴀɴᴅ, D. (Ed) Evaluation in Practice, Driffield, Nafferton Books.

Wᴀʟᴋᴇʀ, R. (1982) 'The use of fiction in educational research', in Sᴍᴇᴛʜᴇʀᴛᴏɴ,
D. (Ed) *Evaluation in Practice*, Driffield, Nafferton Books.

Wᴀʀɴᴏᴄᴋ, M. (1970) *Imagination*, San Francisco, CA, California Press.

Wʜɪᴛᴛᴀᴋᴇʀ, R. (1989) 'Who knows', in Sᴀɴɢᴇʀ, J. (Ed) *Teaching, Handling Information and Learning*, Boston Spa, British Library.

Wɪɴᴄʜ, P. (1958) *The Idea of a Social Science*, London, Routledge and Kegan
Paul.

Wɪɴᴛᴇʀ, R. (1986) 'Fictional critical writing', *Cambridge Journal of Education*,
16, 3, Michaelmas.

Wɪᴛᴛɢᴇɴsᴛᴇɪɴ, L. (1953) *Philosophical Investigations*, Oxford, Blackwell.

Wᴏᴏᴅ, M. (1989) in Sᴀɴɢᴇʀ, J. (Ed) *Teaching, Handling Information and Learning*, Boston Spa, British Library.

Wᴏᴏᴅs, P. (1979) *The Divided School*, London, Routledge and Kegan Paul.

Zɪᴢᴇᴋ, S. (1991) *Looking Awry: An Introduction to Jacques Lacan through Popular Culture*, London, MIT Press.

Index